The Intimate Desert

The Intimate Desert

Walter Collins O'Kane

Illustrations by C. M. Palmer, Jr.

THE UNIVERSITY OF ARIZONA PRESS
Tucson, Arizona

About the author . . .

WALTER COLLINS O'KANE, a Northeasterner, has written these delightful first-hand observations from many years of making his winter home in the Southwest desert region of the United States. He founded the Department of Entomology of the University of New Hampshire and served as Head of that Department, and was awarded an Honorary Doctor of Science degree from Ohio State University. His many scientific affiliations include: Entomologist, University of New Hampshire Experiment Station; Entomologist, State of New Hampshire; President, New Hampshire Academy of Science; President, National Plant Board; and President, American Association of Economic Entomologists. Among his writings are other books pertaining to the Southwest, including *Sun in the Sky* and *The Hopis — Portrait of a Desert People.*

THE UNIVERSITY OF ARIZONA PRESS

S.B.N. 8165-0188-2
L. C. No. 71-76989

My gratitude

to the late Leslie N. Goodding,
resourceful botanist
and identifier of little-known desert plants;

and to Madeleine Jones,
interpreter of illegible writing
and surmiser of an obscure word's intent.

W. C. O'K.

Preface

All through my life the outdoor world, near and remote, has made its repeated appeals for visits and exploration. A footpath in a woodland urges that I come with it and discover what lies at the hidden end. Mountain trails point to the surpassing views that must await the climber who stands on their summits, and some of them win their appeal. Distance is no barrier, but rather increases the strength of the attraction because of remoteness.

The desert country of the Southwest is in itself an invitation and a challenge. It is a world of its own. Everything that exists within its borders lives a life that continually faces necessity, not merely preference. In softer regions there may be choice without pressure. In the desert, pressure accompanies choice and enforces its way by penalties.

Plant life displays this fact everywhere. On trees and shrubs unassuming buds disclose their capacity to change and become unexpected thorns. Twigs themselves grow rigid and sharp. Animal life, possessing the ability to move elsewhere and thus avoid trouble, displays less drastic response but is not immune.

Throughout the long centuries of desert existence, plant life, immobile, has been obliged to make adjustments, to adopt expedients, to accept restrictions, to use endless protective devices. In their amazing diversity these measures form an array no less absorbing to explore than the unhampered original. Thorns have their own story. Bitter leaves can be a guide to life. Roots that remain close to the surface of powdery-dry ground have a meaning. Elaborate flowers borne on miniature stems reflect necessity. The challenge is endless. The extent of country to be explored is boundless.

To observe the endless adjustments, to appreciate the protective devices, to witness the interplay, to illumine the desert life, to find the unsuspected and the overlooked, this is the objective of this book.

WALTER COLLINS O'KANE

Contents

The Intimate Desert

Day by day, month by month,
as I have traveled about
in the desert country,
my constant companion
has been my wife,
Dorothy Braley O'Kane.
The two of us, she and I,
are the "we" of this book.

W. C. O'K.

Introduction

The vast Southwestern United States includes within its sweeping boundaries great arid regions that we often speak of as desert, although the word does not mean the barren sand deserts of the old-fashioned school geographies. When we visit these Southwest desert regions, we find single mountains, mountain ranges, impressive canyons, far-flung foothills, endless reaches of lower ground. We find magnificent space, extending for hundreds of miles from east to west and from south to north. Where streams descend winding canyons and sometimes continue across broad valleys, we find endless combinations of trees and shining water, with rock walls for background. These are the scenes that we all seek to carry away with us on color film. This is the desert's vast and impressive side.

But the desert has another side. Everywhere, as we visit the region, we have all around us the life of the desert. In the valleys and across the foothills, in the canyons and on the mountain slopes, plants grow that are as unusual and interesting as the characters in a play. Unfamiliar animals have their homes in the midst of these plants. Birds that are distinctive fly across the open spaces. There is no end to the array of characters, large and small, that we find on the desert stage.

Inevitably the occupants of the stage — plant and animal alike — live in a world of special and constant adjustment to their surroundings. They must have moisture, in some form and in some degree, and they must have food, whatever its nature and source. They must have progeny to continue their line, and the progeny in turn must have opportunity for success.

These requirements have prevailed and have been met through countless generations. The very existence of the actor on the desert stage is in itself proof of success. Beyond any question, trials and hazards have accompanied the life of the actor. They have shaped the course of development. The plant or animal that you see in the desert is the product of a continuing struggle. It represents a life of drama.

You do not need to search far to find examples. Walk across an open space surrounded by desert vegetation that is shoulder high. Presently you are likely to discover your course beset by plants that are armed with punishing thorns from crown to base. Some member of the cactus tribe bars your way. If you investigate one of the plants and find a wide-spreading network of roots just beneath the surface of the ground, you may be sure that these are intended to catch any droplets of rain that may fall and transmit them to the plant's storage chamber. If you search further you may discover that the storage chamber is filled with material that will hold water but will refuse to let it drain away if the chamber's surface is ruptured. The plant is an example of a successful adaptation to overcome adversity.

If you discern another cactus, clad in a glistening maze of thorns, slender as the finest needle, and if your shoe touches a joint of the plant that lies on the ground, you will find that a dozen of the needles have attached themselves to the leather. They do not penetrate, but they are unbelievably sharp and are barbed.

Not far away you may find a heap of desert trash, the home of a pack rat. Obscurely an opening at ground level leads within. Beside the opening lie two or three short joints of the same needle-bearing cactus. Unbelievably, the pack rat has carried them to this place in his mouth. Not far away another plant of the same kind bears a tunnel-like nest of grass in the midst of a tangle of thorns. A bird has selected the place as a safe location, inaccessible to climbing enemies.

On a rocky slope a cluster of thick and sharp daggers, a foot long and radiating from a common base, are waiting for their year of fulfillment. Already they have waited for more than a dozen years while they stored food within their substance. They will wait for a dozen more, or perhaps two dozen. Then all at once, almost while you are watching, something gives the signal. A tall stalk shoots up, perhaps to a height of fifteen feet. At its upper end a candelabrum of blossoms opens. They bear their seeds. Now the tall stalk and the branching arms grow brown and hard. Down below, next to the ground, the thick daggers slowly die. A century plant has lived its life, has borne its seeds. Now will come the new generation that a fortunate seed among the thousands is bringing into existence.

All through the desert, on mountain slope and in valley, in the sand of a wash and on rocky outcrop, adventure and drama are unfolding. The setting is different from that of other regions, where more moisture favors life. In those regions, as we all know, rivers flow through deep fertile ground. Here in the mountains and valleys of the desert, as in easier regions, there is a wealth of life, but it is specialized. The occupants of the stage, countless in their numbers, are enacting a drama that is vital in its import and rigid in its requirements. In the midst of the vastness of mountains and canyons, the actors live their lives.

This is the intimate desert.

They Crossed the Border

We were watching a young duck who was trying to take off from a small pool beside our road and was finding his runway too short. The place was far to the south in the desert country, not many miles from the Mexico border. Across that border in the course of untold centuries, some animals and some plants had made their way. The country on the two sides is similar.

The young duck finally succeeded, but in the meantime another episode was developing. An armadillo emerged slowly from the grass and very slowly headed for the sandy road. Steadily and slowly it proceeded to cross the road. Its tapering, armored tail dragged behind it, leaving a mark as straight as a ruler, as if the tail were the Finger of Time, expressionless, unemotional, impersonal.

The armadillo might well represent Time, extending back to remote ages. The armor of bony plates that covers its body is a reminder of huge creatures that once roamed the earth and carried about with them the same kind of

4

protection. Others of that remote period left behind them records in the rocks.

South America is the present-day preferred home of the surviving armadillo and its relatives. The one that we have in our own North America is widely distributed in Mexico, and has found a home in the southern areas of states that border on Mexican territory. In its spread into a new region it finds a river no serious obstacle. To begin with, it can swim if need be. Furthermore, if the stream is not large, the armadillo can cross by walking on the bottom. To do this it simply swallows air enough to last it for the crossing.

In our desert country the armadillo occupies only the regions where it can have the sandy or loamy ground that is to its liking, and where the ground is not likely to freeze. In suitable soft ground, it makes the burrows that serve as its home. In the end of a burrow, in the midst of a ball of grass, the female bears a litter of four youngsters.

Strangely, the members of a litter are all of the same sex. This comes about because all are derived from a single egg. Within the body of the female the egg divides, and in turn the results of the division again divide. Thus the members of a litter are "identical" quadruplets.

Before they are many weeks old, the youngsters begin to take on the standard characteristics of an adult. Presently each is encased in armor. Across the back are nine plates, joined together by flexible, leathery strips. When the owner chooses to roll up in a ball, the plates serve as protection, except at the owner's sides. One plate projects over the animal's head. The tapering tail has bony plates on its upper surface.

The head tells the story of the animal's feeding habits. It is prolonged in a tapering snout, which can serve to root up soft ground and bring up ants or wireworms, grubs or termites, spiders or scorpions. Any of these will serve. To secure them the forager makes use of a long and sticky tongue. Its jaws have no biting teeth, only a few short and rounded pegs at the back end. Presumably these may be useful for crushing a small lizard or anything larger than a spider, but most of the items of food, such as ants, are delivered by the tongue and need only to be swallowed.

To prepare any promising ground, so that the long snout can turn up food, the armadillo uses the strong claws on its front feet. These can plow a furrow. Also they can rapidly dig an emergency burrow when danger threatens. When this happens, an armadillo is transformed from a slow-moving creature to one that can run and dodge. It is as if the approach of danger turns the time clock further along, bringing forth the speed of later periods in earth history. The animal needs the transformation, for its eye-sight and hearing are not keen, and the approaching coyote, or javelina, represents an epoch in which speed and aggression were established and perfected.

The broad bed of a wash that we happened to visit was flat and sandy, the kind of surface that would easily register animal tracks. It had been doing just that when we found it and explored it as far as the sand continued. There were scores or hundreds of tracks, all alike in shape and character and differing only in size. The animals that made them must have been a band that included adults and youngsters. They must have been active, scurrying around this way and that across the flat, sometimes exploring the earth banks.

A farmer, examining one of the tracks, would say it had been made by a pig. This would be true, but there was a difference. The track of a pig usually shows the imprint of the dewclaws back of the pair of hooves. The tracks in the wash showed only the hooves. The creature who made the tracks walked on his toes.

The animal was the native American pig, called a javelina, sometimes called a peccary. In Mexico it occurs widely and abundantly. Across the border toward the north it is present in the mountain regions of the southern Arizona desert, and in a few places in adjoining states. It is partial to thickets of mesquite or cactus, where it can run and dodge, and thus escape from its slower-footed enemies who need more room in their pursuit. It likes the open bed of mountain washes which have steep banks where cool places may be found in hot summer weather and warm places in winter.

The javelina is an unmistakable, active citizen, traveling about in loose bands of a dozen or more, covering considerable territory in its movements, but favoring places that are to its liking. It seeks and needs access to water, which will supplement whatever moisture may be present in the food that it consumes.

As you watch a javelina when it has been disturbed, and as you note its manner and actions, you have the feeling that this animal is a one-time domestic pig, modified in the interest of an active and wild life in rough country, and with due regard to speed when need be. Its body is compressed from side to side. Its head is large, with a long and pointed snout, ending in a flat disk, useful in rooting. Its neck is heavy and short, to go with muscular strength and activity. Its legs are somewhat short and seem not to be flexible. When in a hurry, it seems to run in a stiff-legged way. Its tail is so small and short as to be almost invisible. Its body is covered with stiff brownish-gray hairs, which

Javelina

change to light gray, like a collar, at the base of its neck. On its back, from head to rump, it has long bristles, which it can erect when angry or alarmed.

Becoming alarmed is nothing rare in the javelina's life. When something scares or upsets a band, they will take off in various directions. Although their gait is stiff-legged, they can cover the ground rapidly, in spite of obstacles. When the alarm is over they get together again, and this is the point where they may become angry instead of scared. Sometimes, though not often, a band may attack the supposed cause of the alarm, and with their sharp-edged teeth they can be dangerous. All that can be said with certainty is that they are unpredictable. They are nearsighted, and rely on their sense of smell.

A host of other animals besides the javelina depend on the sense of smell, widely possessed and active. Through it, danger may be avoided, and notice served to enemies and friends. On its back the javelina has a musk gland, provided with an opening like a low nipple. This is under voluntary control. When the animal exerts pressure on the gland, a musky secretion is emitted. Applied to a low branch under which the owner passes, it serves notice to any creature that may follow.

The food of a javelina is as varied as the desert itself. Lizards and other small animal life, berries of desert shrubs, beans of mesquite trees, acorns of oak trees, all these are used. With a snout that is specialized, the animal roots up the ground and secures anything edible beneath the surface. Cactus joints, especially those of the prickly pear, are in order. The clusters of spines on a prickly pear pad seem to be no effective deterrent. Everything is chewed up and swallowed. The moisture content of a prickly pear is especially in order.

One product of the desert, rich in moisture, the javelina passes up as a rule. The barrel cactus is too well guarded by its long and heavy spines, recurved like a fish-hook. Occasionally even this serves, when the barrel has been tipped over, and the javelina can work into the unprotected lower side.

In wooded country at the base of a mountain we had prolonged visits with another animal, one that drifted north from Mexico at some indeterminate time in the past. South of the border it is called, as a rule, the chulo. North of the border the same name prevails in various places, especially toward the south, or in Spanish-speaking areas, but in other places the name is coati, pronounced co-ah-tee. Whatever the name, he is an interesting animal, odd in appearance but engaging in his ways. As you discover when you make his acquaintance, he is related to the familiar raccoon, though not at all like him in some aspects of appearance. In fact, he seems at first a completely different animal.

A coati looks as if some of him were intended for some other animal, and is not the proper size and shape. His body is covered with a grizzled coat that is neither fur nor long hair, yet is well-fitting and attractive. His head is

Coati

prolonged in a snout, which is turned up at the end. His jaws are narrow, and the upper part projects beyond the lower part. In fact, in order to drink any liquid, he must immerse a part of his face. The end of his snout is a pad of gristle, suitable for rooting in the manner of a pig.

His legs are odd. Although they are of medium length, the hind pair seem to be a half-size too big. His hind feet especially, appear to be a size too large and long. Since he walks flat-footed, the off-size is noticeable. On soft ground his track shows his long foot print and the imprint of heavy claws. But his tail is the feature most in evidence. Its length is about equal to the entire length of his body, head and all. The tail is not bushy, but is long and cylindrical, covered with fur and faintly marked with rings. As the coati goes about his travels, his tail is likely to be held upright. In fact, if a band of coatis are crossing an area covered with low bushes, all that is visible may be the upright tails. On the other hand, if a coati has taken a seat on a rock or ledge, he may sometimes use the tail as a prop.

Surprisingly, the coati is an agile animal who easily scampers up a tree. If he wishes, he can jump from limb to limb or from tree to tree. His long tail serves to balance him. On his front feet he has long, strong claws, which, although not hooked or sharp, seem to assist his arboreal adventures. In his expeditions through trees he is on the lookout for small birds and especially for nests that contain eggs or young. He seeks also any insects large enough to be worth while.

But his search for food is largely on the ground. With his large front feet, armed with strong claws, he rakes and furrows the ground. With his flexible nose, provided with a tough pad, he stirs and plows the loosened soil. In this way he turns up all sorts of prizes, from grubs to tubers, from mice to lizards. Supplementing these he finds other supplies above ground, such as fruits and berries. And where the country is rocky, he can turn stones with his over-sized feet and thus discover hidden lizards. He is an odd animal. But it seems that his outsize oddities, from feet to long tail, have their advantages.

A company of coatis, young and old, visiting an open space in the forest, were like a community group from town, engaged in a Fourth-of-July picnic.

The first to arrive were five or six grizzled oldsters. They came single file, their bodies partly hidden by low bushes, their long tails erect, the tip slightly inclined. They were followed by a dozen more, who might belong to the next generation. Last came youngsters, ten or twelve of them, scampering about as soon as they reached the opening, running full tilt this way and that.

Meanwhile the oldsters, taking no part in the scampering, began to search the forest floor for the bits of woodland food which were an essential part of the picnic. Others, soberly inclined, began to do the same. One or two youngsters followed their lead, but a sort of holiday spirit seemed to be in the background and to bubble up. Nowhere was there any crowding or ill humor.

A youngster, wandering off a few yards, caught sight of the strangers watching, and instantly climbed a tree a dozen feet for a better look. Two or three others did the same. But the observers remained motionless, and curiosity was soon satisfied. The oldsters and middle-aged paid no attention.

Presently the picnic was over, and everybody left for another open space in the forest, oldsters in the lead, a mixed group following, and one or two competent members bringing up the rear.

Perhaps it was members of the same expedition, perhaps a different group, who visited a forested area in which the cottage is situated that is occupied by the observers who saw the picnic. There were twelve coatis in the new visit. Six of them were full-grown, six were youngsters. They congregated on and around a tree-stump where food had been spread out for birds. The stump was next to the cottage and under a window.

The top of the stump was not large enough for all twelve of the visitors, but this did not lead to quarreling or other sign of ill-will. They simply crowded together, as many as the stump would hold. A hollow in the stump was occupied by two, a youngster and a full-grown, who managed somehow to find enough room for both, and who sought and found the small bits of grain that had dropped into the hollow in the midst of stones. Two others climbed an adjacent tree, looked things over, and presently returned. A full half-hour was occupied by the visitors in their diligent search.

As for the human observers who watched all this from the nearby window, never had they seen as orderly and diligent an expedition, either among wild animals or among those trained to do their parts on a stage.

The Steadfast

Much of the time, as you travel about in the desert country of the Southwest, you have a mountain not far away as companion. Sometimes the mountain is gashed by a canyon. In the canyon there may be a stream which flows visibly and noisily during the wet season, and which disappears during the dry period, although flowing water still continues beneath the rocks of the canyon floor. Another mountain, possessing no canyon, sends along a hidden flow beneath a valley with unbroken sides.

In the canyon, or in the valley, or on the nearby surface of a terrace that skirts the mountain, you will find trees that are as distinctive in their way as some of the desert animals. In summer they are the welcome sources of shade, sometimes the only satisfactory shade that you can find, unless you climb the mountain to the region of evergreen forests. Summer or winter, they have their own habits and characteristics.

Up and down the desert country two kinds of trees grow, often in one another's company, but having opposite appearance and habits. One is as responsive to the seasons as if it had been selected to represent the progress of the year; the other is unchanging, as if it were solid metal.

Where the desert soil holds extra moisture, cottonwoods find conditions to their liking. Sometimes a stream, descending from a mountain, sets the stage. Sometimes a broad and shallow waterhole is bordered by a strip of moist soil. In these places cottonwoods thrive. They are members of the willow family and are allied to the familiar poplars. The trunk of the tree may sometimes reach a diameter of four feet. The ascending branches, clad in furrowed gray bark, tend to spread out, one from another. The tree is tall and of ample girth. The leaf is triangular in shape and is borne on a long stem.

As springtime comes to the desert, the cottonwood responds with a new dress. The trees that will be producing seeds bear long catkins in which seed-bearing capsules are incorporated. The seeds in a capsule are borne in a mass of cottony down. Trees that will provide pollen bear short, dark red catkins.

With the advent of summer, the trees are fully clad in leaves, lustrous green on the upper surface. With the coming of fall, the dress of the trees goes through a new transformation. In the course of a few days the green changes to gold, and the whole tree becomes a warm and shining globe. Two or three weeks later, when frosty nights descend on the desert, the sequence comes to an end, the leaves are dropped, and the framework of the cottonwood is revealed.

Meanwhile the companion trees near by, the evergreen oaks, make no appreciable change from the beginning of the year to the end. Their small and leathery, dark-green leaves, oval in shape, seem as if permanently attached to the twig. The individual leaf does in fact mature, and in due time is discarded, but there is no display of autumn colors. The tree remains unchanged and fully clad. Its strong framework of curving and heavy limbs is unrevealed.

In character of wood the two companions are as unlike as in their dress. The limbs of the cottonwood often break, seemingly in response to their length. The wood is weak. The heavy and compact limbs of the evergreen oak are strong and resistant, as if made of metal.

Billets of firewood derived from the trunk and limbs of the evergreen oaks, often called liveoaks, are unlike anything else ever seen or heard of in the firewood world. To their credit they are excellent performers, burning with steady, glowing heat, remaining alive overnight within a cover of clean white ashes. But they are a world to themselves, unlike cordwood that has been sawed to the desired length, then split and stacked in a long pile, so neat and smooth that it will hold its form without bracing. In the world of the liveoaks a pile of firewood is an aggregation of individuals, no two remotely alike. Each piece has had its own experiences, and each relates some of its adventures, by its length and shape, its surface, and the holes in its substance.

A short and thick section of a trunk defies anyone to determine its age by counting its rings, because these have been host to woodboring ants, which have made their home in the heartwood. Another section of trunk, although missed by the ants, was visited through all its life by winds that twisted it until its fibers were rent asunder, giving way to strange and angular cavities. The winds obliterated the rings as completely as did the ants.

A section from the base of a tree, growing next to the ground, flares out until it is like the round and heavy pedestal of some gigantic column. A piece of heavy limb makes a sudden change of direction. Where another tree would have brought about the change by developing a branch limb, this one chose the difficult way and produced a right-angle turn. In contrast, another section, which elected to branch, apparently exhausted itself in the effort and now comes on the scene as wood long since dead. Here and there the pile contains long pieces not thick enough to be worth sawing. Only an over-sized fireplace could be big enough to find room for these.

The aggregation is like an assemblage of actors from a stage, each with his own curious makeup and costume.

Along with the cottonwoods and the evergreen oaks, another tree grows, which is equally fond of an area well provided with water. You find this tree all around you when you explore a canyon. It will be on hand although the supply of water is all beneath the canyon floor. This tree is as water-minded as its companions, but whereas a cottonwood freely adopts the characteristics of its group, the rounded form and upright stature, and whereas an evergreen oak could be identified in the dark by its adherence to the rules, the third member of the company is always different from its fellows. It is a sycamore.

A sycamore seems to be unpredictable. Visit a canyon and you will find trunks leaning to right and left, to north and south, toward the water and away from it. Limbs branch from trunks at every angle and continue on a strange course. Smaller branches start at an upward angle and turn down. In all the canyons, in all the mountains, no two sycamores are alike, or conform to any plan.

But in a different frame of mind, visit a canyon, travel its length from outlet to source, and see the white forms all about you. Note the great, strong trunk that leans over a pool in the canyon floor, where crystal water from springs and from melting snow reflects the white column above it and gives it a background of deep blue sky. Note how a far-flung limb reaches out toward the lichen-covered wall. Travel a few steps farther, and discover a new and different pattern of white and blue and rock wall. Journey to another canyon and travel its length, and then to another. Never will you find two designs that are alike, and never will you discover one that is other than rewarding in its own special way.

Week by week in our travels we have followed a little-used unpaved road that is bordered by flat and mostly uninhabited desert. We have found there desert wildlife that prefers its own world. We have found the traces of a vanished human occupancy and the long-ago records of its ceremonial life. Now we have found something recent. Like the setting for a story of intrigue and mystery, the desert that borders on the road harbors a native citizen who is known by an assumed name.

In the margin of a desert wash, where the ground receives adequate moisture, a tree grows that in many ways looks like a willow. It may reach a height of fifteen or twenty feet. It tends to spread out in an irregular way, matching the growth of some willows. Its trunk is dark and rough, with bark that is likely to show imperfect channels. As it comes into leaf in early spring, after a winter of leafless twigs, it seems all the more to belong with the clan of willows. Its leaves, long and narrow, have an appropriate character. When it drops its foliage in the fall, the similarity of trunk and limbs continues. So the tree is spoken of under its assumed name, the desertwillow.

But in the meantime, after spring gave way to summer, something revealing was taking place. The blossoms that appeared on the twigs were not at all the catkins of a willow, not anything that the willows would ever claim. They were shaped like orchid flowers, with curving tubes ending in a flared and scalloped opening. The tubes were lavender-white and were decorated with broad round markings, which were brown or sometimes purple.

Since these blossoms revealed its true character, the tree could not retain its assumed name. It is in fact a catalpa, related to the shade trees of the North and East which often are planted along streets and in private grounds. Its true name would be the desert catalpa.

When summer is ended and the flowers are gone, a further characteristic remains, to deny the correctness of the assumed name. The flower is succeeded by a long and slender seedpod, again a reminder of the catalpa. By the time winter is over, the pod has split lengthwise. Within it lie many seeds, neatly packed. Each pair of seeds is covered with a glistening silk garment with a long fringe at the end, a silk parachute to carry the seed to some other desert wash where the bank is moist and the ground is mellow.

There is nothing halfway about the smoke tree of the Southwest. It believes in going the limit in whatever needs to be done.

Its home is in the hot, sandy desert, preferably in the border of a broad and shallow wash that has been swept by summer cloudbursts. If luckily it has become established, it may have come to rest in the middle of the wash, where it must withstand succeeding floods.

Since the tree must meet the extremes of desert heat and dryness, and at the same time hold fast to whatever moisture it already contains, it has dispensed with any substantial foliage. What leaves it retains are no larger than a fingernail and are only sparingly distributed over its bare branches — so few leaves in fact that the tree seems to wear almost no clothing. To keep life continuing at all, the angular branches are gray-brown, taking the place of leaves.

Since the tree must produce seedlings, which will continue the race, it blooms profusely. Its blossoms are gray-blue, like the color of smoke. At the blooming time in early summer, the blossoms immerse the tree in a haze of their own color, and this is the reason for the tree's name.

The seeds that follow the blossoms are ready to germinate without delay, as soon as they are mature. All that they ask is further rain. But the same rain can be too heavy and can be their undoing. Since nearly all the seeds have fallen to the ground not far from the parent tree, and since the parent may be in the bottom of the wash, in the path of a rushing torrent, most of the seeds will be carried away. The survivors will be those which lodged on higher ground and which made haste to take root.

At this point the smoke tree comes up with its thoroughness of preparation. The young seedlings, during the beginning of their life, until they have had time to become established, are provided with full-sized functioning leaves. Later, in due time, they can get along with the small substitutes no longer than a fingernail. It is as if the parents, themselves threadbare, insisted on providing luxury for the next generation.

In mountain valleys near the Mexican border, a pine tree grows that has a twofold claim on distinction.

The tree grows only in certain mountains, and nowhere else. Yet it is no weakling. It grows to a height of sixty or seventy feet, with a straight trunk that may be two feet in diameter. Its heavy bark is so dark as to seem almost black. Deep fissures in the bark are reddish, as if they were creases in sunburned skin. The branches are few and heavy, and the twigs are stout rather than slim or flexible. The wood of the trunk is hard and heavy. In every respect the tree is strong, a fit companion for the well-known ponderosa pine, which is found with it and which grows in extensive forests over many miles of mountain country.

A second claim of this tree to distinction lies in its characteristic needles. They are unbelievably long, sometimes measuring fifteen inches or more, the longest needles anywhere in all the western country. In contrast, the ponderosa pine carries needles that are five or six inches long, and the southwestern white pine has four-inch needles.

Years ago the tree was christened Apache pine, an appropriate name, since its home is in the rugged country where the Apache Indians had their stronghold. As you look at one of these trees you can see a third claim to distinction. Not only is the tree named for an Indian tribe, but in its character, its rugged strength and its tall and straight form, its dark colored bark and its windswept crown, it is a reminder of an Apache warrior himself.

An orderly company of trees occupies a level space near the foot of a mountain. They are about the size of dwarf apple trees, and are spaced apart as if they might have been planted. They were in fact grown from seeds, which were carried by birds or the wind, and they are evenly spaced in accordance with the soil moisture in the area where they stand. Farther down the slope the ground carries more moisture. Here the tree growth is like a tangled thicket, each member crowding its neighbors because each one seeks space. Still farther away a broad terrace is occupied by creosote bushes, which can get along with gritty ground that seems bone dry. In two or three isolated spots on the surface a single tree stands, hugging the ground, its lowest limbs half buried in windblown sand.

In each of these places the tree is the one called mesquite, either the kind called honey-mesquite or the one known as screw-bean because its pods curl up tightly and look like a screw. Each kind has sharp and short thorns where a leaf stem branches from a twig. Each can send down a tap root to an almost incredible distance to find water. Each is an example of the resourceful plant life that survives and thrives in a desert country.

Mesquite trees cannot offer the juicy fruit that an apple tree provides, but they have other attributes. Since time immemorial, their properties and possibilities were understood and appreciated by Indian tribes of the desert. The bark of the tree was pounded and made into a rough fabric. Gum that exuded through a cut in the trunk was used in mending pottery. From the sap of the tree a black dye was obtained. The juice from a wounded limb was the base of a thick decoction that served as a treatment for sore throat. The seedpod provided not only its store of beans but also the pulpy substance in which the seeds were embedded, and this became a confection. A further gift of the tree proved to be a prize for the white settlers and remains a valued attribute today, for the blossoms of a mesquite provide pasture for bees, and the honey which the bees produce is of rare flavor.

Visit a region of the desert where sand dunes form. Note that a dune slowly travels, as strong winds move the sand grains. Learn that mesquite trees may be buried by an advancing dune. Then sometime you will find that a tree, long buried, is coming up to the light, its wood preserved by the dry sand. That wood, you will learn, is prime fuel. The trunk and limbs of a mesquite are hard and heavy and will burn well and long.

Night Highway

On a trip afoot one day, we came upon a narrow track made by horses on their way to a pasture somewhere. The trail must have been in use for a long time, for it was cut deeply. It was narrow, no wider than the space required for a slow and plodding walk. The cleancut sides drew a sharp line through the desert vegetation, permitting no grass roots to exist, denying the adventures of the roots sent out by neighboring shrubs. The bottom was soft sand, continually freshened and stirred by the animals as they returned to their home.

The course of the track was long ago determined by the flat terrace itself. Where mesquite trees tended to grow near one another, the trail zigzagged in their midst. Where a clump of catclaws stood in the way, the track circled around them. Where a bed of prickly pears had spread from a rocky ledge, the path avoided both ledge and cactus. Where a gully crossed the flat, the trail made a shift in direction to reach the gently sloping area near the head of the gully. Where a rock outcrop seemed to bar the way, the route found and used a sunken course between upthrusts of the rock itself.

Every morning, before the horses had started for a distant pasture, the bottom of the path contained a narrative written in sand. In an hour or two the pages of the book would be destroyed, but for a brief time, while dawn gave way to sunrise, when the native citizens of the desert had retired to their homes, the book was untouched and open.

A jackrabbit, out for early breakfast, found the path proceeding in his direction, hopped into it, continued for a few bounds, and then returned to the unrevealing desert floor. A fox, arriving early, before the jackrabbit's passing, followed the route of the path all the way to the distant pasture. A pack rat, on his way to his home in a prickly pear patch and carrying an ancient buckle from an old harness, descended to the bottom of the path. Chancing to follow it for a yard or two, he came upon a bright link from a small chain. Dropping the buckle he picked up the link and hurried on to his pile of rubbish in the midst of the prickly pears. A mouse, traveling alone and leaving in the sand a line of little footprints like embroidery, reached safely the shelter of a small burrow in the bank of the path. Just before the horses came, a roadrunner, following the track and marking the sand with unmistakable prints, leaped out to visit a well-liked place on a fencepost for a sunbath. The narrative of the highway came to an end, until another night.

Every few days for several weeks we followed the path and read what we could of its story, always in certain knowledge that we could decipher only a small part of the history recorded in the sand. If somehow a human being, visiting in the desert country, could be granted in the hours of darkness the vision that he has in daylight, a whole world of animated life would surely be disclosed.

The fox that leaves its clean and precise footprints in the sand would become a living creature, keen of nose and attentive to slightest sound, an embodiment of self-sufficiency. Circling on hushed wings an owl would draw a pattern against the starry sky. The deer that crossed the trail would linger in an open space where grass and browse offered food. Out from the hidden world of darkness the desert would bring forth the other half of its busy life.

All through the daylight hours, the observer can see the evidence of the smaller life that inhabits the desert but seldom is visible by daylight. Everywhere there are little tracks in the sand, tracks no larger than a fingernail. They lead here and there, crossing and recrossing, as if those who made them had been visiting. The owners are nowhere to be seen, for this is not the time when journeyings could proceed in safety.

In the midst of the tracks stands a bush with tangled, rigid branches, armed with sharp stubs. Beneath the bush is the entrance to a tunnel. Near the bush there are other small entrances, the convenient side doors and back doors. What quarters lie beneath, what galleries and living room, storage rooms and nursery, no one can know. Marauding animals cannot invade. Above ground the interlaced branches are walls and bars. Beneath ground the tangled roots, extending many feet, are locked doors.

The desert is garden and playground, wheatfield and cornfield, dining table and granary. The bush is stronghold. The chambers beneath are sanctuary.

Anyone who has occupied a cabin in a woodland anywhere in the North American continent has learned that the premises are likely to be sought by other would-be occupants, especially when winter is approaching. In the stillness of the night you hear the noise of gnawing. It sounds as if the animal were as large as a porcupine. The beam of a flashlight discloses a small creature with bright eyes and large ears, sitting on a shelf. Its small paws are white, and so is its shirt-front. Its long and slender tail is softly furred, brown above and white beneath. Other members of the clan to which it belongs, the whitefoot mice, are entering or trying to enter every conceivable cabin, every available retreat, in regions all across the continent, including the desert country of the Southwest.

You will not see them in daylight hours, for their activities are confined to darkness. In the dust of cattle-tracks, or in the fine sand bordering a desert wash, you can find their footprints, which are in pairs because of their hopping gait. Unless these small creatures are driven indoors by storms, they are abroad every night in search of food. The seeds of grasses or taller plants are a standby, supplemented with almost anything else that is edible. To tide themselves over bad weather or cold, they accumulate supplies of food in crevices and small hollows, though their stores are not extensive. They simply go hungry if necessary when times are hard.

Somewhere the whitefoot has an insulated retreat, which serves when nights are cold. He collects grasses and any other soft materials that are obtainable, shapes this material into a ball, lines the inside of it with the softer substances, and moves in. If there are nearby dwellings or other buildings, they serve as a possible location. If nothing so complete is within reach, a hollow log or a cavity in the midst of rocks will serve. Wherever the nest may be, it signifies home territory, a certain area that is private property and that will be defended against intrusions by other members of the whitefoot clan.

Always night-time is activity time for the whitefoot. In daytime potential enemies are on the watch — foxes, coyotes, weasels. The best defense against these is darkness. As for owls or others that hunt at night, only caution can avail.

In one of our visits to the night highway we saw tracks that seemed new in the sand. We followed their faint trail across the flat to a house occupied by a collector of curios — a pack rat. The house looked like a mound of trash. It reminded us of some ancient curiosity shop, or the dusty quarters of an oldtime dealer in antiques. The fact that the owner apparently liked to collect strange objects seemed to be in keeping with his premises.

Evidently the choice of location for the mound was influenced by security, as if the owner had treasures to guard, as well as his own safety from marauders. Since a patch of prickly pear cactus was available, the mound was built in their midst. Since thorny shrubs surrounded the house and overhung it, so much the better.

The material used in making the mound was literally anything that could be found on the desert floor within a range of a hundred feet or more. Clods of earth, sticks, thorny twigs, rocks, pieces of bark, old bones, dried-up droppings left by some desert animal — anything would serve. Over this trash the owner had deposited cactus joints, especially those of the cholla, with their sharp and barbed needles.

In his nightly trips in search of food, the proprietor of the house brought back with him anything that he could add to his premises. Now and then he found something unusual — an old harness buckle, a bottle cap, a fragment of a mirror. If his journeys took him to an occupied dwelling into which he could find entry, his discoveries might be especially rewarding. Within reach he might find a shiny silver spoon, a pair of shoes from which he could remove the laces, a collection of coins, or even a watch. These prize discoveries he could silently remove to his own quarters, one by one. These were his special curios. Since he is abroad only at night, he has several hours in which to work undetected.

In the course of his trips he is likely to run across the usual objects of the desert floor, bits of trash, and to pick up one of these while on his way. Once inside an occupied dwelling and ready to carry off a coin or a watch, he must discard the bit of trash in favor of a more unusual item. So it comes about that he is accused of offering something worthless, such as an old bottle cap, in exchange for a silver spoon.

The curios that he finds are placed somewhere in the base of his mound, like the objects in the dusty window of an old curiosity shop. If he finds something bright and shining, he is in luck, better off than many of his desert neighbors.

Like his neighbors, he has constructed a house which is more than it seems to be. The trash that makes up the surface of the mound and most of its bulk is protection. The cactus joints add to its efficiency. Deep within the heap lies the real home, a globular structure made of soft grasses. Devious passageways at ground level lead to this. Their outer beginning is inconspicuous and uninviting. Cactus joints and other thorny material guard the real hidden opening. Since long-used trails lead from an opening to foraging grounds, protective joints of cactus may be placed next to a trail, especially near its beginning. Curios that the house owner acquires are likely to be placed in the midst of the protective possessions.

From the appearance of a pack rat's house, it might be surmised that the owner would be unkempt and untidy. But the opposite is true. While he is called a pack rat or a traderat, he is completely unlike the rat that infests city surroundings. He is clad throughout in short and silky fur, which is light and buff color on his underparts. He has large ears and large brown eyes, and he is provided with long whiskers, which can help him avoid obstacles as he travels in the dark. Except when youngsters are making their start, he lives alone in his house. His premises are like the old dwellings on the mesas in the Southwest desert country. Once his house has been constructed and fortified, it may remain in use for many years. If the owner dies, a new occupant, perhaps one of the children, moves in.

There is no difficulty about food supplies. The surrounding desert within a radius of a hundred feet or less provides whatever is needed, including mesquite leaves and seeds, desert grasses and the pulp of cactus. From these resources the house-owner garners reserve food, which he can store in his house for winter use. As for water, he may not need any, since the moisture in some of his food may be all that he requires. And always there are the curios that he or his predecessors have added to his premises.

In another direction and in different surroundings, a broad mound that we saw, actively in use, would equal in size the home of the pack rat, but would be unlike it in other ways. Its owner, a kangaroo rat, would have no use for cactus joints decorating the surface or for a devious entrance. Like the pack rat, he is probably out at night securing food, but his return to home quarters needs open going and a chance for speed.

His mound is usually in an open, level space. It is perhaps two feet high and two or three times as broad. Opening into it are four or five holes. If you walk over to the mound and strike its smooth surface with the flat of your hand, you are likely to hear a thumping noise inside. The place is occupied.

Because the mound and the holes are large, you know that the owner is a kangaroo rat, well-named because he travels in the same way as the big Australian animal. The mound is his own private quarters, not an apartment house. The openings are large because he needs an adequate entrance that he can use quickly and easily if he is pursued by an enemy and must find shelter without delay. If you could trace the galleries within the mound, you would find them extensive, probably occupying more than one level.

The owner is an entertaining fellow, with interesting ways. In all of his traveling he uses only his long and strong hind legs, hopping easily when in no hurry, making prodigious jumps when emergency arises. The end-joints of his hind legs are broad and provide a handy stool when he sits down. His front legs are small, but they serve almost as if they were hands to pick up items of food and to do the chores that the hind legs cannot undertake. His body is compact and is clad in a coat of soft fur. His head is large and his eyes are big. He has fur-lined cheek pouches for transporting the seeds and other food that his front legs pick up for him.

His long tail, longer than his body, is an effective possession. On its tip is a tuft of hairs, which help the tail to function as it streams out behind him when he jumps. With this combination the kangaroo rat can steer his course while in the air. If need be, he can change direction after he leaves the ground, and in a succession of jumps can zigzag as he goes. Since he may journey to some distance from his mound in foraging for food, his zigzag and speedy return may be critical. The ample openings into the mound may be essential.

The mound itself is his castle. He shares it with a mate only briefly, during the time when a new generation is in order. The rest of the year he is the castle's autocrat. Although he cannot possibly occupy all the galleries or make use of all the food storage advantages, the mound is his own. Other and smaller members of his clan, content with smaller mounds, may lead a communal existence, using their structure as an apartment house. But not this larger fellow. If one of the others ventures into a gallery, attracted by the possibility of stealing some food, he is met with a violent reception. If sometimes the visitor is large, a fight ensues, both combatants seeking to use their strong hind legs and the claws on their feet. Both are likely to suffer.

Seeds of various kinds are the principal food of the kangaroo rat. Strange as it may seem, there is little inclination to supplement this dry food with water. In fact the reverse is true. If a day comes when there is fog or mist in the air, the owner of a mound is likely to remain in his quarters until the moisture has dissipated. To make up for any moisture deficiency, he shares with some other desert animals the ability to convert the starch in seeds into water. By a bodily chemical process he manufactures his own moisture. To keep his fur dry during wet weather, he follows the procedure used by birds. On his back he has the opening of an oil gland. The secretion from this is used to anoint the fur. If too much anointing results, he takes a sand bath to remove the surplus.

The kangaroo rat does not hibernate, nor does he cease activity and go to sleep in hot weather. Since he is abroad in night hours only, he avoids the direct heat of very hot sunshine. If the temperature rises too high, he retreats to a low gallery of his mound, and if extreme heat and dryness prevail, he plugs up one or more of the openings to his quarters.

His castle is both refuge and stronghold.

One day we found in the sand a pair of round tracks, parallel and close together, each one as large as the footprint of a big dog. They were the signature of an animal and a reminder of an implacable disposition. The animal was a bobcat. The disposition cannot be defined in one word.

Bobcats are present here and there in the Southwest country, although they are not often seen. They do their traveling and hunting at night, and they spend the daylight hours lying quietly in some secluded place where they can have all the sunlight that comes their way and can be unobserved. If the preceding night's hunting has yielded poor results, or if their resting place happens to be disturbed, they move into the open, or may start out to seek more food.

Their hunting, night or day, is largely on the ground, not in trees. They can and will climb on occasion, but ground level usually serves. Down there they find rabbits and ground squirrels, and sometimes a bird, such as a quail, feeding on the ground. Their hunting procedure is to approach stealthily and to pounce when within range. They do not usually attempt to run an animal down, for their bounding gait is not swift, and they are soon out of breath. The fact that they have good hearing and eyesight helps them in their silent approach. The territory over which they range may amount to four or five square miles, but only a part of this is covered in a hunting trip. It is their method to go slowly and to search fully every small hollow or thicket. When a prospective animal has been detected or suspected, the hunter is willing to wait motionless for hours, leaving the next move to the victim. The method of a domestic cat, when out on a hunting trip, is parallel.

The bobcat is of course much larger than a domestic cat. Its fur is tan color, with dark spots. On the tip of each ear it has a small and slender tuft of hairs, an abbreviated edition of the conspicuous tuft of the Canadian lynx. Its home den is some rough and inaccessible cavity in the midst of rocks. In that retreat its young are born, one litter a year.

One time a friend of ours found a young bobcat, not yet half grown. The youngster was soft and appealing. Carried home it was installed in a cage. All went well for a few weeks. Then adulthood came to the young animal, and everything was different. Its ingrained disposition came to the surface. A violent antipathy to any human being developed. If the owner of the captive, or anyone else, approached the cage, or even came into sight, the occupant snarled and hissed. Its attitude was implacable. Any calming words or gestures merely made the outburst worse.

Evidently the two round tracks in the sand had not been made by an animal like a friendly kitten.

High up on a canyon floor, a small area of sand, no more than a yard in diameter, had caught a single footprint. The bounding animal had placed its other front foot on the stony ground next to the sand. But although only one print could be seen, the identity of the animal was certain. The print was about as large as a man's hand, or a little larger. It showed a heavy central pad. Around this were the distinct imprints of four well-marked toes. The footprint was the signature of a mountain lion.

That mountain lions exist in the desert country of the Southwest may be surprising, but understandable. In various parts of the region the tumbled groups of mountains, covering many miles, rising to impressive heights, unpenetrated by an extensive road system, may well be expected to harbor some of the lithe and powerful animals.

The sheer weight and strength of a mountain lion, combined with its agility, are enough to account for the respect in which it is held, even though it is not inclined to attack human beings. A full-grown animal may weigh a hundred pounds or more. Its long cylindrical tail is characteristic. Its head is armed with strong jaws and teeth.

The food that it seeks depends on the territory it covers. A deer would rank first as desirable food, but deer can run faster than lions, and must be captured by stealth. Smaller animals, such as rabbits, raccoons, and foxes, are welcome as food. Sometimes domestic animals, such as sheep or cattle, are victims. To secure a domestic animal, the hunter may need to travel many miles, but a mountain lion is accustomed to travel. Its ordinary range may be fifteen or twenty miles.

The single footprint that we found in the sand might mean that the animal was in the midst of a pursuit, or might signify only that it was following its accustomed travel habits. As it turned out, the visitor was on its way down to the farming country at the foot of the mountain. Two days later a rancher visited a cattle pasture that he owned, which extended to the mountain slope. He discovered that one of his animals had been killed. Tracks at the scene told the story. It was done by a mountain lion.

The Rain Savers

If a survey were to be made among the plants of the Southwest country, to see which groups are especially resourceful in meeting desert conditions, a place would surely be won by the cactus clan.

As anyone would agree, the lack of adequate moisture is the start of plant troubles in the desert. If the rainfall were as ample as that of the Central States, or the East, everything else would more or less straighten out. Probably there is plenty of plant food in the ground. The wind may blow hard at times, but it is able to carry the soil away only when the ground is dry. Dust storms and sand storms do not come along when the ground is moist. Animals that like to browse on plants would choose, if they could, plants that are tender and inviting. The growing season in the Southwest is long. It could produce two lots of plant growth. But it needs plenty of rainfall. In the lack of this, a native desert plant must adopt expedients to produce even a limited growth.

The cactus clan begins at the beginning. Their procedure is to capture whatever rain may fall, however limited, and to store it for whatever future needs may require. The container for storage is the plant itself. The structure may be no larger than a marble or may be a column twenty feet tall. It may be a connected series of cylinders, or a flat receptacle like a pad, or a substantial affair like a barrel. It may have a smooth and continuous surface or may be fluted in the interest of easy expansion.

In any case, the container is living substance, manufactured by the plant. It develops and grows in accordance with the design of the plant and with due regard to the surrounding conditions. It remains alive and functioning throughout the life of the plant. It can enlarge its own storage capacity on demand. A human visitor, even one who has had engineering training, would be hard pressed to offer anything quite the equal of this.

In accordance with cactus procedures, a container is usually green, the same green as that of leaves on other plants. In fact it is serving in the same way as a leaf. In the cactus world, leaves have been largely eliminated.

To protect the storage unit and its moisture content, the tribe possesses an elaborate variety of thorns. These again are a part of the living substance. They are likely to grow in radiating clusters from a common base, and thus to protect intervening areas. They may be barbed, and thus a more threatening deterrent. Some of them may be curved at the end, like a fishhook.

These are the familiar aspects of the cactus tribe. But there is another aspect, below the surface of the ground and less familiar. Since a cactus plant is built to store its own supply of water, not to seek supplies that may exist deep in the ground, it does not depend on a deep taproot. Its root system spreads far and wide, just beneath the ground surface. The system is prepared to seize upon whatever rain may fall, transporting as much as possible to the storage chambers, where the moisture serves the plant through periods of drouth. A cactus plant leaves nothing to chance that can be attended to in advance.

Among all the varied examples of plant life in the Southwest country, the giant, exclusive of the trees, is surely the saguaro cactus. Growing to a height of forty or fifty feet and standing secure on its foundation, it is a noteworthy structure in the world of plants.

The engineering requirements involved in the saguaro's growth were bound to be considerable. Its root system is an intricate mat, situated near the surface of the ground. From this mat rises the central column, with no supporting buttresses. By itself the column must meet all the strains that may develop, including those of unusual windstorms. The strains may be increased by side branches arising from the column, although a branch on one side is likely to be balanced by a similar structure on the opposite side. The weight of all this growth may reach ten or fifteen tons.

The central column, the key to the engineering design, contains within its substance fifteen or twenty vertical rods, extending from the base of the column to the upper part. Each rod is an inch or more in diameter. The set of rods is arranged in a circle, embedded in a tenacious substance that helps to maintain all of them in an efficient position. Outside of this combination comes the shell, designed with vertical ridges and valleys, like flutings. This in turn reinforces the strength of the column. The ridges carry the plant's armament of thorns.

The substance within the shell, especially the core that lies inside the rods, is adapted to storage of water. When rains arrive, the water is captured by the mat of roots and transported to the storage chamber. If the rain is heavy or prolonged, the storage material may need more room in order to expand. The shell meets this need by increasing its diameter. The flutings lend themselves to this requirement, since they can permit decreasing the depth of the valleys between the ridges or altering the shape of the ridges themselves. In order not to waste any of the moisture that has been collected and stored, the surface of the shell is coated with wax.

Building and arranging all this structure takes time. A saguaro is a plant of slow growth. Its juvenile period, before it develops the ability to produce blossoms and to bear seeds, may occupy forty or fifty years. Its entire life, from its small beginnings to its decline, may extend to two hundred years.

When it is ready to enter its blossoming stage, it produces at the top of the central column, and at the end of each branch, a circle of rich, cream-colored blossoms, like a garland. It does this only once a year. A blossom has a brief period of activity, opening in late evening, closing in the following mid-morning. It is succeeded by a fruit which is three inches long and an inch and a half in diameter. As the fruit ripens, it splits lengthwise into segments. The outer surfaces curl back, disclosing the content of the fruit, a brightly colored red pulp. Within the pulp lie small black seeds. Birds come to the pulp and carry the seeds to new places, where in due time a seed may germinate and start a new saguaro on its long life and on a further demonstration of effective design.

Among all the members of the cactus tribe, the prickly pear seems to have an appearance of self-sufficiency, a sort of complacency, that sets it apart from the others.

It does not make use of an intricate manner of growth, such as that of the deerhorn cactus, with branches that seem baffled and unable to proceed further in an orderly way. It does not lose a joint here and there. It does not require that the desert provide it with unimpeded room all around, which it can utilize for its own exclusive purposes and thus develop a colony of its own kind.

The prickly pear gives the impression of a forthright plant. Its broad pads, with their moist and succulent interior, are displayed for any and all animals to covet, and attack if they can. Where there is plenty of room overhead, it raises pad after pad, higher and higher, as if it flaunted its treasures. If there is room on either side, it sends out a row of pads, each new one attached to the margin of the preceding member, often each new arrival a precise duplicate in its size and relative position. The fruit that follows a blossom occupies a place on the rim of a pad where seemingly it would be vulnerable, but there are enough of them to offset losses. A pad breached by a thirsty animal will be one near the ground. Other pads, higher up, stand above a thorny understory.

If you are interested in the amount of moisture stored inside a pad, find a stick with a sharp-pointed end. Thrust this through the leathery surface of a pad. Work it around to stir and macerate the firm pulp within the pad. Thrust it on through the farther surface, making a hole on that side. Withdraw the stick and you will find that no liquid flows out of the holes, even though the surface of the stick is moist. The pulp inside contains a suitable store of liquid. The plant is too efficient a conservator to permit any liquid to escape from any hole that pack rat or jackrabbit might contrive to make in a pad's surface.

Since the moist pulp in a pad would itself be sought by predators, further protective measures are provided. The smooth flat surface of a pad is protected from gnawing by its very flatness. There is nothing on which eager teeth can lay hold. But even this is entitled to added protection, and so the suface is provided with long radiating spines, which come in clusters. The clusters are spaced an inch or so apart. The nose of a small animal cannot reach the surface because the spines make a complete barrier. The edge of a pad would be vulnerable, but here the spines are more closely arranged and give the added protection that is needed.

In its utilization of a possible location for its growth, the prickly pear is resourceful. If an area is occupied by rocks so near together that seemingly there is no room for any plant growth, the situation is acceptable to the prickly pear. Other plant adventurers will avoid it, but not the prickly pear. Narrow spaces provide an entry for roots, and nothing else is needed. Beneath the rocks a store of moisture may be found, a supply adequate for any needs. In due time the area becomes a prickly pear garden, in which rocks become merely the background for a display.

Not far away an open territory, which has no rocks,

is occupied by a company of deerhorn cactus. They grow as high as your waist or your shoulder, and there is no unoccupied ground in their midst. In fact, some of the largest seem to have passed their prime and look bedraggled. In one direction there is further territory to be exploited, but in another there is a barrier which they cannot cross. A long ledge, rising a foot or two above the ground, crosses the region. Prickly pears have seized upon crevices in the ledge, and have erected a row of multiple green pads. In their luxuriance they seem to exhibit an inviolate self-sufficiency.

A cactus group that seems to have special traditions is scattered through desert territory. In the view of various human visitors who have had considerable personal experience, the traditions might reasonably be changed. The group is the one known as the chollas.

In countless open spaces a cholla grows as if it had been designed as the embodiment of dejection. Its needle-covered joints are slender, they tend to droop, as if the plant were the victim of premature old age. They bear yellow fruits which appear to be harmless but in fact are covered with small and sharp spines, too inconspicuous to be noticed. The plant is called the deerhorn cholla, or sometimes the staghorn cholla. When it grows in the neighborhood of the prickly pear, which is the picture of well-fed self-sufficiency, the contrast is striking.

The chollas have another member that meets traditions in a way that is not only different but, from the human point of view, extreme. Often it is called the jumping cholla. It cannot actually propel itself, but it accomplishes results which suggest its name. Its joints are short and are so completely covered with myriads of needle-like spines that they seem to have greater diameter than they really possess. The tips of the needles are encased in a sharp, microscopic sheath, which comes off and remains in whatever the needle penetrates. To make the picture complete, the joints are so loosely attached that they come off at a touch. If a barbed needle penetrates a substance, whether human flesh or anything else, the entire joint lets go. Often detached joints lie on the ground beneath a plant, as if they had indeed been propelled by the parent cactus.

Wherever they are, the members of the cholla group live up to traditions.

The cactus tribe includes within its world a member that is impressive in a completely different way, a way as different as day is from night.

Several simple columns rise from a single base. There may be fifteen or twenty in the group. Often they stand roughly parallel. Their length varies from seven or eight feet to as much as fifteen feet. The diameter of a column may be six inches. Each column is fluted, with narrow ridges and valleys, and each is softly grayish-green because its flutings carry inconspicuous slender and short spines. When the right time of year arrives, pale flowers are borne near the top of a column. Later the flower is followed by a small red fruit, with crimson pulp. Its surface carries many spines, but these are easily brushed off.

In the region near the Southern border, where these plants grow, you can see groups of the columns here and there across the desert. You will not notice any thorns, for they are not prominent. You will not see the pale blossoms, for they are open only in the night. What you see will be banks of cylinders, like the pipes of an organ, for this is the organ pipe cactus.

Roadrunner

Travelers by Air

When a rangy brown bird, as tall as a chicken and provided with a crest, appears suddenly beside the road and goes streaking away on a dead run across the desert, you can be sure what it is without referring to a bird-book. The second half of the roadrunner's name is properly descriptive. Although he does not always follow a road in his swift departure, he surely can run.

Among all the many birds of the desert country, the one that to us has the most engaging personality is the roadrunner. Day after day, as we travel about, usually in a car and moving slowly over some little-used road, we are always on the lookout for a roadrunner in the border of the road ahead, or somewhere in the nearby desert area. The reason for our interest is not because we want to add a name to a list of birds seen and identified, but because we can count on some unexpected and original performance, which we do not wish to miss.

A roadrunner has his own procedures. In some of his ways he follows the usual program of a bird, but most of his habits are different. Like others, he can fly, but he does so only when he chooses, and not in sustained flight high above the ground, or anything like soaring. In his procedure, flight is an adjunct to running. His first dependence is on his strong legs. If he happens to follow a course which leads across a steep-walled desert wash, he sails out, bounces from the ground in the middle of the wash, and sails to the top of the bank on the farther side, all of this like one prolonged jump.

Like other birds, the roadrunner builds a nest; like many nests, this one is made of sticks in the crotch of a tree. For the roadrunner, seven or eight feet from the ground, or perhaps ten, is enough, being beyond the reach of coyotes. A juniper is likely to be chosen as the site. The nest is lined, but not with feathers or soft grasses. Dried desert material suffices, possibly with the addition of a snake skin. The roadrunner is not a society bird with sophisticated ways. Occupancy of a nest is likely to be prolonged, because the routine of egg-laying may occupy many days. With these ways as background, the roadrunner proceeds with his own special bag of tricks.

As if in appreciation of desert sunshine, especially in winter, he likes to begin the day's activities with a prolonged sunbath. This is neither perfunctory nor haphazard, but like a ritual. Standing on the top of some strategic eminence, he fluffs out all his feathers until he looks like a round ball. His long legs are doubled up and concealed under him. He remains in this position for an extended period, perhaps half an hour. During this time he does not wish to be disturbed, and discourages interruptions.

If he is in ranch country, where fields and pastures are fenced, his choice of an eminence for his sunbath may be a fencepost, preferably one near the ranch buildings, especially if they house farm animals. This means possible food supplies. Normally his food is provided by the desert, and includes such items as grasshoppers, spiders, centipedes, baby pack rats, cactus fruits, horned toads, and especially small lizards. These he is always hunting and securing with his strong bill. But the addition of waste grain from a feed-yard is welcome.

In fact, he appreciates food from a ranch kitchen. Once he has established a handout, he is likely to make it a regular event. Every day he shows up at a certain hour, and always he is punctual. If he is due to arrive at ten o'clock in the morning, he shows up at ten by the clock. His timing is accurate. Sometimes a small group of occupied dwellings, situated in desert surroundings, gives him a profitable circuit from door to door. This he cultivates. At a given hour and minute he makes his appearance and proceeds with his calls.

Out in the desert he prefers an area where low-growing trees and thorny bushes give him protection. In this he can dodge and run, faster than a fox or coyote, while at the same time he is safe from attack by air. From his stronghold he goes out on his round of adventures. Always he can run like the wind and can dodge and disappear. As a chaser of lizards he has daily practice. He is interested in anything that moves. Golfers whose course lies next to desert country may discover that a golf ball dropped in the rough has seemingly disappeared for good. A roadrunner who lives near by has never-ending sport in chasing golf balls. He enjoys also running in front of a slow-moving car on a rough desert road.

The build of a roadrunner is made to order for his ways and desires. His legs are long and strong, his body compact. His tail is long and is used in up-and-down steering of his course. His neck is long, and often it is held straight out in front when he is making time. On the crown of his head he has a crest, which he can elevate when he chooses. The toes of his feet are like two V's, one open toward the front, the other toward the rear. No doubt this arrangement is useful in running. Since the toes are alike toward front and rear, the owner's track in desert sand does not tell you which way he was going. In a legend of the Hopi Indians, a roadrunner saved them from a pursuing enemy, because the enemy could not tell from the tracks which way to go.

If you have discovered a roadrunner near by, in the midst of desert grass and bushes, and if he has not been disturbed by your presence, a first-class variety-show is likely to follow.

Coming out from behind a bush, but remaining partly hidden by tall grass, he inspects you. Like a performer about to appear on the stage, he stretches out his neck to its full length and eyes you from head to foot. Erecting the tuft of feathers on the top of his head, he steps out in front of the bush for a moment and makes his entry. His long and smooth tail is gracefully raised and lowered, like the gesture of an old-time actor.

In a moment he retreats into the concealment of the tall grass, but only in order to find an acceptable place for a further stage entry, like a performer answering a curtain call. If you move along slowly, he keeps pace with you. Alternately the crest on his head is erected and depressed. With every appearance in the open, his tail is smoothly raised and lowered, in a dignified and courtly way. He is in no mood to go elsewhere, but seemingly is enjoying the situation and the opportunity to display his talents. Now and then he pecks at some crumb on the nearby gravel. Although he seems to find nothing worth swallowing, he goes through the motions of discovering food. Presently you have an uneasy feeling that you ought to provide him with some reward. If you had with you a cracker, for example, you could give him something in response to his entertaining program.

In the midst of his routine he occasionally turns away and takes a few steps into the bed of grass. But in a moment he reappears in another open space and resumes his gestures with his expressive tail. Always he keeps a bright eye turned in your direction. All this continues in unbroken and unhurried deliberation.

Eventually the performance comes to an end because you have other affairs on hand. But you are the one who rings down the curtain. Apparently to the roadrunner the show is only well started.

Like a party of youngsters, all properly dressed and out for a walk, a company of Gambel's quail crossed a stony open space near us. They might well have come from some private school, where expeditions for nature study are a regular procedure, each student wearing the insignia of the school, and each well trained in good manners.

The first member of the company to reach the open area hurried across to the farther side. Singly and in groups of two or three, the others arrived. Some lingered for a few minutes, interested in what they found next to the adjacent road. Others made haste to catch up with the first arrivals. None paid any attention to the strangers.

Presently the early arrivals were scattered about in the midst of stones, small and large. Three or four took up a position side by side on the highest stone and quietly observed the human beings watching them. There was no alarm, no trace of nervousness.

In their motionless pose, their uniform was plainly to be seen. Each one wore a buff waistcoat, snugly fitted and extended up to the throat. In the center of the waistcoat was

Gambel's Quail

a smooth black disk. On the head a jaunty feather rose gracefully and curved forward. These items, the black disk and the jaunty feather, were like the insignia of their school. The narrow stripes on their wings were shared with other schools, and were somewhat similar, though not quite the same.

In a few moments the friendly inspection was over, and the observers joined their fellows, who were searching hollows in the midst of stones — a proper nature study. None of them paid any further attention to the strangers.

It seemed to us that two small birds of the desert country must have made an agreement to respect the rights of each other. The smaller of the two, a bird no larger than an English sparrow, is the desert resident called the elf owl. He appears very small to be a member of the tribe of owls, but that is his family. The other bird, only a little larger, is the pygmy owl.

Sometime in the past the elf owl found a nesting place to its liking and adopted its discovery. If you visit a region where the saguaro cactus grows, you can see a small round hole in an occasional giant stalk. This is the work of the Gila woodpecker. The hole is the entrance to a vertical cavity which the Gila has excavated for a nest. If you are lucky, you may catch sight of a small face looking out of the hole, a face that quickly disappears as its owner retreats. The cavity is one that the Gila has abandoned, and the tenant is the elf.

The pygmy has different ways. The saguaro cactus has no appeal to him, but an unused woodpecker hole in the trunk of an evergreen tree is a suitable choice. Equally acceptable is a former woodpecker site in an oak or a sycamore. In the lack of these, a hollow in a stump will be adequate.

When dusk comes and night begins, the elf leaves its retreat in the saguaro and starts out on its foraging round. Its food is the diminutive life of the desert, grasshoppers when in season, beetles of various kinds. If these are not available, ants will take their place. The usual food for owls — the mice and small birds — seems to have no appeal. As it wings its way in the darkness, the elf softly whistles an almost warbling call. When dawn comes and daylight begins, the elf is back home in the saguaro.

About the same hour in early morning the pygmy sets out and continues through full daylight. It does not call out in warbling notes, but its wings make a whistling sound, which perhaps serves the same purpose as the cries that larger hunting owls send echoing through the trees. In spite of its small size, the pygmy is a hunter in search of animal life, and it is willing to cope with creatures as large as itself.

A Baby Elf Owl Wakes Up

Sometimes it is able to surprise a bird. Sometimes it can get the best of an unwary small squirrel. If these cannot be had, it seeks one or another of the larger insects, but always it is an active, resourceful hunter.

When the day is over and dusk begins, the elf has its turn again. Once more the little owl calls out a quavering warble as it flies.

Following a path that skirted an area taken over by cholla cactus, we saw a bundle of grass, large as a football, anchored in the thorny structure of a cholla. Hundreds of slender, glistening needles surrounded the bundle. Fibers of grass were interlaced around the thorns, fastening the structure securely in place. No wind could dislodge it; and no marauder, coming on foot or by air, could invade its armored security.

A hundred yards away, beyond the region of chollas, a mesquite tree extends scraggly branches. One of these, longer than the rest, ends in a tangle of twigs, each one bearing sharp thorns along its crooked length. In the midst of the tangle a bundle of grass is anchored, the duplicate of the one in the cholla cactus. Again the grass fibers are woven around the twigs. Nothing can dislodge the structure.

Beyond the mesquite, an area of desert grass is dotted with the unkempt trunks of yuccas. Some of these carry rigid flower stems, three or four feet long. One of the stems dates back to the preceding season and bears a cluster of dry seedpods, arranged on short branching stems. In the midst of these rests a grass bundle, like those on the cactus and mesquite. Again the bundle is securely anchored. This time there are no thorns, but the dried flower stem is unbranched, and the cluster of seedpods is six feet or more above the ground. The thick base of the yucca carries an array of long and slender leaves, like spears, which project in every direction and occupy a space as large as a bushel basket.

When you examine one of the bundles of grass, you find an extension on one side, like a short and thick neck of a gourd. A tunnel leads through the extension to the center of the bundle. The snug space inside is lined with feathers or other soft material. The grass fibers are the walls and roof of a small room, and they are so well placed and arranged that the walls, the roof, and the floor, can withstand storm and assault.

As might be surmised, the builder of the nest is a wren. But it is not a small bird, such as the familiar house wren.

Cactus Wren

It does not carry its tail upright. It is not a noteworthy song-ster, such as the winter wren. Its established and well-earned claim to fame lies in its remarkable nest and the extraordinary site for the structure. Nearly always, when the time comes for nest building, it chooses the intricate thorny heart of a cholla cactus, and so it bears the well-earned name of cactus wren.

As if to offset its relentless character, a catclaw is often the home of one of the desert's interesting birds. The little gray titmouse with a yellow cap, the verdin, is likely to choose a catclaw for its nesting site. In the midst of thorny twigs, near the outer end of an upper branch, the adventuring bird constructs a roofed-over home. The inner part of the home is soft grass. The outer part is largely the adjacent thorny twigs themselves. In this fortified shelter the youngsters are raised. On a neighboring twig they perch when outside their home. In the shelter itself, after the youngsters have matured and left, the mother is likely to find a resting place when not on the wing. In a similar shelter, on the same tree or one near by, the male has his quarters, not as carefully constructed, but serving a purpose as a fortified and safe retreat.

We would not have imagined that a woodpecker nest, intact and complete, could be removed from the trunk in which the bird had done his excavating. Nevertheless it can be done in the desert country.

The Gila woodpecker, who lives in the Southwest desert, often finds the saguaro cactus trunk attractive. The column may be twelve or fifteen inches in diameter and fifteen feet tall or more. It is armed with thorns, but these are good protection from enemies. The Gila digs a hole through the surface at some point to its liking, continues the hole a short distance into the softer inner part of the trunk, then turns downward and makes an enlarged cavity that may be a foot or more deep.

All this is in accordance with usual woodpecker procedure. The cavity is true to form. But that which follows is a product that would not develop in the trunk of a forest tree. The cactus responds to the excavating by coating the entrance hole with a liquid which becomes hard. It does the same with the inner surface of the cavity. The entire affair, from the entrance to the bottom, becomes a sort of unit that will last for a prolonged period.

In the passage of years, perhaps many years, the cactus becomes fully mature and eventually dies. A strong wind knocks it down, and when it lies on the ground its disintegration proceeds. Someone exploring the desert comes upon the fallen trunk, discovers the woodpecker hole, and is able to separate the fibers of the trunk, thus securing the nest. Removed from the trunk, it has somewhat the appearance of a giant wooden shoe, all enclosed except for the entrance.

In making use of the saguaro, and in countless other ways, the woodpeckers of the Southwest country have had to meet many special situations. In the Plains states, the Mississippi valley, the Appalachians, and toward the north, woodland area is extensive. Trees grow that are adapted to traditional woodpecker life. Their trunks are productive hunting-ground for food, and useful territory for excavations and home sites. The woodpecker form reflects this. A vertical surface is acceptable and right. Toes are arranged to make use of such a surface. Tail feathers, ending in a rigid point, can serve as a bracket when ascending a trunk. All is in logical order.

But relatives who live in the Southwest may have had to modify their ways. In the upper areas of the higher mountains, forests await, but these areas may not always offer food of the right kind, and the climate that prevails there may not always be acceptable. Regions farther down, which border on the real desert, may be the available territory, and so the choice narrows and the traditional ways need adjustment.

An aspect of this involves walking on a flat, level surface instead of one that is vertical. This may be awkward for the bird, and may seem so to the human observer, but when securing food is the objective, it can be done. On the other hand, if the need is to excavate a hole for a nesting site, something better than a flat, level surface is called for, and here the low-lying desert offers substitutes for the orthodox trunks of maples and oaks, beeches and pines.

One of the substitutes, the saguaro cactus, raises a column that is for all the world like the trunk of a tree. It is an armored trunk at that, with rows of thorns. It has a surface that is firm while at the same time adapted to chiseling with a woodpecker beak, and it has an interior substance that will hold a nest cavity. But the saguaro occupies only a certain territory, extensive but not universal. In any case, the Gila woodpecker has appropriated the use of saguaros, and not many other birds live there.

The big lily that grows with a large trunk, and is called a Joshua tree, seems less suitable than a saguaro, but nevertheless it is used on occasion for nesting. But Joshua trees, too, grow in only a certain region, and cannot meet all the needs of woodpeckers.

A native tree, the mesquite, is widespread, but it has drawbacks. If its trunk could be excavated with woodpecker equipment, the entrance hole would be near the ground and vulnerable. Its limbs have no notion of following a straight course, but twist and turn. It has sharp thorns, but these would not protect trunk or limbs.

Apparently the recourse for a woodpecker would usually be the trees that grow in the mountain canyons or the border of washes. This situation does not seem much like the easy world of an eastern forest; but there are many woodpeckers in the desert Southwest, so it must be acceptable.

From his perch on a lookout, high above our heads, a big bird launched forth and slowly circled. He did not soar on rising air currents, as might a vulture, but moved under his own power, using the strength of his strong wing muscles. As he circled he surveyed the desert beneath him, searching for whatever animal life it might offer.

His body and wings seemed almost black. His neck and head, in contrast, were a shimmering bronze that glowed in the sunlight. This was the clue to his name, the golden eagle, cousin of the bird whose head is clothed in close-fitting white feathers, the bird called the bald eagle. Unlike the bald eagle, the golden eagle is a hunter of forest borders and foothills, and is not inclined to favor the banks of streams or the shores of lakes. Over his territory he must be able to fly strongly and swiftly. His wingspread of seven feet is almost as great as that of the bald eagle.

As master of broad inland skies, the golden eagle has his personal hunting domain, which may extend for several miles. This is his kingdom. Other and lesser birds may share their holdings with lesser claimants, may quarrel over boundaries or yield to the pressure of rival claimants. The golden eagle is too commanding to feel pressures. His home territory is well defined, as if it were enclosed in an invisible boundary of the air. A desirable area, once established, may be occupied by golden eagles for many generations, as if it were a principality handed down through a series of years.

The hunting grounds of a golden eagle must be relatively open. Since the bird is a big one, it needs room for its flight, especially in pursuit of an animal. If the animal can easily dodge under shelter, as in a region thickly grown to bushes and trees, the chase is baffled. In the Southwest the jackrabbit is often the victim of a golden eagle. The jack is large enough to provide a meal, and there are many jacks. Also the eagle may sometimes hunt by stealth, and the dozing jack may never have a chance to exercise his native speed and agility.

A satisfactory site for the nest of the eagle must meet definite specifications. It must be inaccessible to predators traveling on the ground. These are potentially the enemies of adult eagles and inevitably a threat to fledglings, not yet on the wing. The site must be large enough to provide adequate space for a golden eagle's big nest, and must be strong enough to support the heavy weight of a nest that has received substantial additions every season for a period of years.

In a country where there are canyon walls, an admirable situation for a nest may be a shallow cave or a shelf, high up on a cliff face. In a region of mesas, the precipitous drop from a high tableland to the country below may provide a suitable site, especially if protected by an overhang of rock strata. In a country that has no cliffs or canyons, the available nest site may be near the top of a tall tree that rises above its neighbors and has strong limbs, well placed for nest purposes. Such trees are in fact the occupied sites in various areas.

The distance from the nest to the hunting ground may be considerable, but all of the involved territory is included in the great bird's kingdom. A golden eagle can cover many miles without seeming effort.

Underground World

In the desert country, wherever you go and wherever you may be, you will see before you the unceasing drama of desert life. If you make a circuit, afoot or in a slow-moving car, and if you repeat this a dozen times, you will find that in the course of each trip you are seeing new examples of desert adventures. Always you are looking for the actors that you saw before, and are speculating on the nature of events that may have taken place meanwhile.

Near the desert cottage that we have occupied at various times, a road leads straight away for ten miles across a terrace. We have followed that road almost daily for many weeks, in a car and driving at a walk. It has never failed to yield rewards. The terrace that the road crosses extends along the base of a mountain. The surface of the terrace is unevenly covered with patches of grass and with low-growing mesquites and other shrubs, intermingled with open spaces where the sandy ground is sometimes bare.

Early in the course of our trip, we left the car and walked about on the terrace. In one part of it we found low mounds, scattered about. They had no apparent orderly relationship. The distance from one to another might be fifty feet or five hundred. If they constituted a town, in any sense of the word, its location appeared to have been determined by nothing appreciable. Narrow paths, three or four inches wide, led from the largest mound, but they seemed to have no understandable objective. Sometimes a path appeared to be directed toward another mound, but it failed to make good its seeming intent. An occasional well-used path proceeded to the border of the road that we had followed but disclosed no destination on the farther side.

That the largest mound was occupied was evident. Two low sides of it were penetrated by six or eight holes, and these entrances showed marks of use. Whether the mound was the property of a single tenant, or whether there might be several owners, and whether these were related, were matters that could not even be guessed. We felt that it would be entertaining to explore the mound.

Some of the holes that led into the mound were large, perhaps six inches in diameter. Seemingly they could admit an animal as large as a fox. But the ground was crumbly, and a hole might easily grow larger with normal use. The occupants were not in the habit of coming out and displaying themselves in their travels. Their foraging for food was no doubt safer in darkness.

But an item of food provided a clue. The definitely larger mound was not only higher but broader than the others. Its diameter was twelve or fifteen feet. The entrance holes were all in its low sides. It looked like a community club or a social center, or perhaps a dining hall.

Within a few yards of this mound we found that a low ridge was occupied by martynia plants, the desert unicorn plants. They had finished their blossoming period and now bore their curious seedpods. A martynia pod is a hard, leathery receptacle, two inches long and a half-inch in diameter. Near one end it bears a pair of slender and wiry prongs, which curve out and around and end in a hard point. The two of them make a circle four or five inches in diameter, with the seedpod in the middle of one side.

Inside each pod lies a store of seeds. Evidently these were coveted by the owners of the big mound, whether a family, a dining club, or a single proprietor. The standard procedure with an ordinary pod would be to carry it into the mound, using one or another of the entrances. But the martynia pod, with its prongs, was another story. Carried by a harvester with his teeth, and making a circle over his head, it would not go through any of the holes leading into the mound. The only recourse was to bite a suitable hole in the pod and remove the seeds.

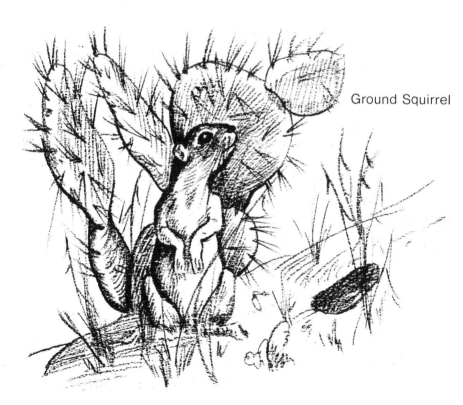

Ground Squirrel

We returned to the car and quietly awaited developments. So it came about that after a while the gray head of a ground squirrel, who was sitting in a shallow depression on top of the mound, was visible from the road. His head was surmounted by a circle of the martynia prongs. Being observed, he gave up, abandoned his prize, and disappeared.

A further look then disclosed the accumulated stores of the dining club, however owned. A bundle of martynias, with horns tangled together, lay near the base of the mound. Their seedpods had not been entered. They must have represented storage for future needs. Another bundle, close by, also with horns interlocked, included pods that had already supplied ground squirrel's desires. Near the base of each pod, at exactly the same spot, was a small round hole.

We did not find out whether similar martynia stores exist in other parts of the terrace. There were no others in the area we visited. But the fact seemed certain that the large supply of nearby plants and the size of the big mound were related. The dining club was popular.

The road that crosses the terrace is bordered on each side by a narrow strip of desert ground, in which grow scattered shrubs and clumps of grass. Scanning this one day as we drove along, we came to an open space in which there was a small mound of fresh earth. The mound was no more than a foot in diameter and a few inches high. A yard away there was another similar mound.

When we came back the following day, more mounds had come into existence. In one of these we could see a small hole in the middle of its surface. We did not see the excavator, but because of the nature of the work that was being done, we were confident that the owner was a pocket gopher.

Not far away other similar mounds appeared from time to time. They were the visible evidence of a concealed underground world, which is like a fourth dimension. The occupants of that world have their own system of highways and byways. As need arises or inclination urges, they extend the system, opening hidden roads to new objectives, to food supplies or to new living quarters. They build connecting links and establish safety retreats.

On another terrace we found an opening at the surface of the ground, giving access to a narrow path in the midst of rocks and desert vegetation. The route led to another opening, situated at some distance. The path looked well trodden, as if it were in frequent use. We could only guess the reason for its existence. Perhaps it was the visiting route between two colonies or two families. Perhaps the ground between was too rocky for tunneling, and a surface journey was the only way. Perhaps an underground connection would be undesirable, because the young offspring of a family were required to find and maintain their own home and not to depend on their parents.

Few creatures of the outdoor world lead as secluded a life as does the pocket gopher, or could do so if they desired. He does not leave his premises to visit the open country. Down there lie hearth and home, food and nursery, all of the activities involved in existence. Among familiar animals only the moles seem to rival his way of life.

The mound of fresh earth that appears here and there is likely to be the terminus of a gallery excavated in search of food. For the most part underground roots, tubers and the like, are the gopher's food supplies. Finding them means continual tunneling, and this in turn means more or less accumulation of surplus earth. Eventually the surplus is pushed up out of the way.

From the gopher's point of view the main galleries of his underground world are ample. They are large enough for easy passage, and probably of sufficient diameter to permit turning around. They lead to special quarters for special purposes, to storage rooms for surplus food supplies, to what might be called a living room, to a suitable place where the young gophers are born and started on a gopher career, and to a small room that serves as a toilet — a room that presently is sealed off, giving way to a new cubicle. All of

Pocket Gopher

this represents a world of darkness. As might be expected, a gopher's eyes are small and inefficient.

The branch galleries to secure food serve only the one purpose. Therefore they are likely to be only as large in diameter as the gopher's body, too constricted to permit turning around. The only way to return to the starting point is to go backward. This is a familiar and long-standing situation in the gopher world, so familiar that the digger in the burrow can travel backward just about as easily and rapidly as forward. His short tail guides him.

From our point of view a gopher, with his compact body and big front claws, is not a handsome animal, but after all, he never offers himself to be viewed and admired.

Across the road from the dining club and the martynias, the terrace was rougher ground. Over there, in the midst of occasional rock outcrops and gullies, we found a different kind of hole, which had a strangely wide and flattened open-ing, and which had no mound around it to betray its presence. Evidently its owner was a badger.

All through the Southwest country the badger is often found among the animal population. Because of his way of life, he is not likely to be seen, but his work tells the story. He is not a small animal, since his body length is twenty-four inches or more, and his weight is fifteen or twenty pounds. But his legs are short, and he seems flattened to the ground, head and all. The whole effect arises from the fact that he is built to burrow in the ground, and to do this rapidly and efficiently.

When in search of small animals that make up his food, he does not try to run down a scurrying squirrel or a bound-ing kangaroo rat, but seeks gophers or ground squirrels, or other animals that often are found beneath the ground sur-face. He pursues them by digging. If he himself is threatened by an enemy while he is on the surface, he promptly digs his way down and disappears, so rapidly that he seems to vanish before the enemy's searching eyes. To do this he is suitably designed and equipped.

Badger

His body is clad in dense, durable fur. His tail is short; it is not a thing that can get in the way. On the surface the badger does not stand notably above the ground, as does a swift animal that can make time. He is close to the ground, ready to dig. His legs are powerful, and his front feet are equipped with long and heavy claws, which have just one object in life, to dig. His hind feet are less fully equipped, but can help the front feet.

In finding and securing food that is beneath the surface, the badger relies on a keen sense of smell. Where gophers have excavated a series of galleries, the badger who arrives on the scene knows where the occupants are, perhaps a family of them, and can start digging accurately and efficiently. If he runs across a broad mound erected by ground squirrels, with half-a-dozen entrance holes, his survey is quick and his digging fast and accurate. Most of his excavating is done in ground that is free of large stones. This, of course, is the kind of ground that is favored by small burrowing animals. If occasion arises, however, the badger can and will dig in a place where he must remove stones as big as your fist or larger. If he is not going too deep, the hole that he makes tends to be wider than high, conforming to the shape of his body.

When the unusual happens and the badger is seen on the surface, in early morning or late afternoon, he proves to be shy rather than pugnacious.. On his face he has the mark that matches his name — a broad white stripe from his nose over the top of his head, like a badge.

Anyone who has had a speaking acquaintance with a chipmunk in the Central states or in the East is bound to respond to a certain feeling of renewing old times on running across the former friend's cousin in the Southwest. The trees are somewhat different from those in home country, the ground is not the same, but the friendly manner is reminiscent, and the haste to store away any offerings is unchanged. East or West, North or in the Southwest, a chipmunk is an engaging citizen of the outdoor world. He is perpetually busy, is always cheerful, and seems to seek no quarrels with other creatures.

The clan of chipmunks is almost as widespread as the continent itself. Occupying a wide range of territory, living at altitudes ranging from low valleys to high mountain slopes, the tribe includes various groups with different markings. The one that you are most likely to see in the Southwest is less distinctly striped on the body. But he has the typical striped head which is the membership badge of chipmunks everywhere. His tail, though flattened in the orthodox manner, is inclined to be a little bushy. As if aware that he possesses a suitable tail, he likes to wave it slowly from side to side as he runs. He is not in the habit of carrying it straight up while he races across the ground. Since he enjoys climbing trees, he is likely to be seen in mountain valleys where trees find the surroundings suitable. Fallen tree trunks are especially favored for traveling about, since they provide an elevated roadway.

Like all his cousins, the chipmunk of the Southwest has cheek pouches into which he can load small items of food for transport to a storage place. The items thus collected are many and various. They include seeds of all kinds, berries, nuts — in fact anything edible, and especially anything that will remain sound for future use. Seemingly he is forever carrying food to some place where it can be hidden, though of course this activity is increased when winter is approaching. His storage places may be several, including one where he has established his home. With this, he combines others not far away.

Home is always a protected chamber. If the ground is suitable and can be tunneled, as in Eastern territory, the chamber will be a small room at the end of an underground passage. In this the chipmunk provides a soft bed of leaves or other acceptable material. If the ground is rocky, the chamber will be in the midst of underground crevices. In any case it is sheltered and below the usual ground level. In this home he is safe from hawks and coyotes, and in it he rests during midwinter, living on his supplies of stored food.

Sometimes the technical name that has been assigned to an animal is especially appropriate. This is true of the chipmunks, who are classified under the name *Eutamias,* which means good steward.

In another part of the desert, fifty miles or more from the terrace and its inhabitants, we left our car and started across a broad open space of red earth and small stones. We were bound for a hill that was said to yield garnets — not gem material, but stones of an odd crystal form. We did not discover any garnets, but we did find an interesting and unexpected phase of desert life.

In the open space there were many low mounds, a foot or two high. Some of them carried on top a scraggly bush, bearing scant leaves. Others bore only the dead remnants of a bush. Hidden beneath the surface of each of them, a network of roots anchored the mound and prevented it from disappearing over the horizon when strong winds blew. Beneath some of the mounds, small animals had chambers that were their home quarters. You could know of their presence because of the small entrance tunnels at the base of a mound. No tracks on the surface were visible, since the rough and gritty earth did not easily carry the footprints of small adventurers who had set forth in the night.

A large mound that was different from the others occupied a space to itself. Its base was broader. Its sides were marked with irregular hollows, as if the inner substance of the mound had given way. Its top also was caved in, and the half dead shrub that grew there had only a precarious foothold. The mound was in fact all that was left of a once busy community.

Formerly the roots of the shrub on its top were many and attractive. Small desert animals sought the mound for home and shelter, and for the food that the presence of the roots invited. Gradually their galleries and chambers honeycombed the earth. Their work was so extensive that after a while the mound itself was weakened. In time the supply of living roots came to an end. The galleries were no longer usable. The walls and roof of the chambers gave way, and the mound collapsed. Today it is only a reminder of its former size and activity.

Two or three miles away stands a low mountain which once held a store of gold and silver. This also was tunneled. The deposit of precious metals was so rich that in the mining operations, they say, inadequate columns were left to support the roof of galleries. Every cubic foot left for support was worth money. In time the operations proceeded to the point where, apparently, the upper part of the mountain gave way and fell in upon the lower part.

Unlike and yet alike — the mound in the desert, and the mountain.

Fortresses

Week by week, as we travel about in the desert country, we sometimes find ourselves in the company of the desert's version of a fortress. If we are exploring in a car, following a little-used road, we can see here and there in an open stretch of country a compact growth that looks as if the branches of a shrub had turned in upon themselves and produced a ragged, almost solid ball. If we are afoot we will discover ahead of us a dozen or more of these obstructions, perhaps well spaced out, perhaps growing so closely together that a detour is necessary in order to reach an objective.

In some regions the cactus clan, with their myriad spines and their characteristic green color, have taken over most of the available space. But the fortresses are different from any cactus. They are a shrub-like growth, thorny enough but with strong and resistant branches, which display little green color or none at all. On open flats and benches, which have not been occupied by the cactus tribe, the fortresses will be spaced about in the midst of grass-clumps and small shrubs. In any case they have their own way of life, their own form and structure.

Here and there, on the benches at the foot of mountain slopes, we found a type of fortress that seemed to embody everything conceivable in the way of efficient design. It has more than one name, but often is called the buckthorn. After we were acquainted with it, we could distinguish one at a distance, because its thick growth has a bluish appearance. It retains small green leaves all through winter.

The buckthorn is as firmly rooted in the ground as if it were anchored there. Even after some accident has brought its life to an end, it still remains strong and immovable. It sometimes branches next to the ground, leaving no space underneath. It spreads out to a diameter of six or eight feet. It grows to a height of six feet or more, too high to be surmounted by any creature other than an agile, bounding invader.

Immediately above the ground its strong trunk and branches twist and turn and interlace. They continue to follow this design all through the plant's structure. The woody substance of trunk or branch is hard and rigid. No effort can avail to move it aside or untangle its interwoven complexities. At every least turn every branch, from the largest to the smallest, sends out a long and rigid thorn, which is needle-sharp. Since the branches turn and twist, the thorns point in every direction. Since the smallest twig carries a thorny array, the entire shrub is completely armed. No least area of its surface is free, just as no part of its interior is unprovided with punishing spines.

Seemingly the birds know all about the buckthorn. Apparently the cactus wren, which builds a nest in the midst of cholla needles and finds a thorny mesquite acceptable, has no liking for the buckthorn. The verdin, which willingly raises a family in a catclaw shrub, seems to draw the line when it comes to a buckthorn. A jackrabbit, seeking shelter from a hawk, may be unable to dodge beneath the branches of a buckthorn if they chance to hug the ground. A road-runner avoids the armored shrub and trusts to concealment in clumps of grass. Here and there in the midst of ragged creosote bushes, you can see thriving buckthorns, compact and sound.

After many trips to various places in the desert, we chanced to find a shrub which may be entitled to even a higher rank than the buckthorn as a fortress. It is called the allthorn, or often the crucifixion thorn. It is a rounded shrub, usually three or four feet tall, sometimes six feet. Except for a brief period, it is literally and completely one great branching mass of heavy thorns. The actual sharp and stout thorns themselves, two inches long or less, are the twigs. The branches and main stem continue the same heavy and strong design. Early in the season very small leaves, like green scales, are borne; but soon they drop. Clusters of small greenish flowers are carried by the branching thorns; but they are inconspicuous. The flowers are followed by small berries, which are black and equally inconspicuous.

A closely related variety differs principally in the fact that it is taller, reaching the height of a small tree. Like its relative, it drops its small leaves early in the season, and seems to be a leafless mass of tangled thorns.

Just as a military fortress may have other structures near by, which add to its effectiveness, the buckthorn and the allthorn are likely to have a companion. In the course of crossing a desert flat we found the one that may be entitled to top rank. It is an acacia, known as the catclaw. Usually it is a shrub, eight or ten feet high, with widely spreading branches. In some places it grows to the height of a small tree, with a trunk that is four or five inches in diameter. Briefly, in the growing season, it is dressed in leaves; but when its need for dress is ended, the branches and twigs are bare.

When springtime is established, the catclaw adds to its dress a wealth of blossoms. Its flowers take the form of compact cylinders, an inch or two long and a half-inch in diameter. They are pale yellow, and they spread on the air a far-reaching fragrance. Myriads of honeybees respond to this and crowd the yellow blossoms. The nectar which the bees carry home is the source of much-desired honey. This, along with the fragrance of the blossoms and their filmy yellow display, is the plant's contribution to human enjoyment.

A further contribution follows when the blossoms are succeeded by flat and characteristic seedpods. At first the pods are pale brown, but as the season moves along, the color changes to deep red. In their richness they add a decoration which is like a sequel to the blossom display.

Two other contributions have been offered by the plant. The seeds within the pod, when mature and dry, were gathered by native Indians. Pounded to a meal, they were an addition to food supplies. The other contribution is used in modern times. The trunk of this acacia has richly colored wood — the heartwood deep reddish-brown, the sapwood bright yellow. The grain of the wood is firm and strong. Attractive small articles are made from it.

But there is another side. Along its branches and twigs the plant bears innumerable thorns that offset any credit balance. Each one is short and stout, no more than a quarter-inch long. Each one is firmly anchored and very sharp. And each one is curved backward toward the base of the twig or branch, not toward the tip. If you come within grasp of a plant, and any part of your clothing or your skin is caught, you can be released only by deliberate retreat, thorn by thorn. The armament of the plant is like that of an implacable cat. It is fully entitled to its common name, the catclaw.

In countless places an open bench is likely to carry another and different barrier. As you look across the level area, you see what appear to be shrubs, sometimes growing shoulder-high or more, sometimes half that height. They are likely to be spaced apart somewhat evenly, but to occupy nearly all of the room at their disposal. If the ground is moist, they may form an almost solid growth, through which an animal as small as a rabbit would have trouble in passing if pursued. Where there is less moisture, the spacing is more open, and a fleeing animal can dodge and run. In either case these plants are an extensive adjunct to the fortresses of buckthorn, allthorn, and catclaw.

They are another version of the same mesquite that sometimes reaches the size of a tree. They have branched close to the ground, forming no appreciable trunk. They have neither the interlaced spiny armor of the buckthorn, nor the implacable curved thorns of the catclaw, but they are not unarmed. Spines on the older twigs may be short. Those on new growth may be long. In any case the branches and twigs are likely to be stiff and unyielding, and the obstacle, in company with its many neighbors, is a determined barrier.

Another occupant of similar benches is distributed still more widely, for it will grow in any kind of ground, even that which tends to be alkaline, and it seems to thrive in the absence of adequate water. It is called the saltbush. It has no armament of thorns, but it grows so densely that in itself it is a barrier. It begins to branch at the surface of the ground, leaving no space beneath and none above. It is grayish in color, and it looks ragged and unkempt, but it seems to need neither thorns nor a resistant structure. It is an effective supplement to the other fortresses.

Refuge

Many times, through many weeks, we visited a broad area of uneven or sometimes stony ground, grown up to countless clumps of desert shrubs, large and small. In a way we could walk anywhere we chose. Looking at the area from a height and a suitable distance, you would say that it lay open to unlimited exploration. But in the area grew specimens of bluish gray buckthorn which permitted no liberties. In the border of a wash an array of catclaws stood ready to lay hold of your clothes, refusing to let go unless you slowly and discreetly humored the captor, inch by inch. The area was the home of fortresses.

In every visit to the place, early or late, we were invariably made aware of its twofold character. To the human visitor innumerable spots were impenetrable. You could not pass through them or step over them or heedlessly draw too near. They might well have carried a warning sign, "No Trespassing." But to many desert animals, and to birds, they were a refuge, always available, easily used, and well fortified. The low and interwoven thickets were just as important as the taller and thorny shrubs. The combination was the guardian of life itself.

In one part of the broad area mesquite trees grew closely together. We knew that a supply of moisture must be present deep beneath the dry surface of the ground. We knew that the trees had drawn upon their ability to send a taproot far down into the earth.

To the native inhabitants the situation had a further significance. Tightly growing mesquite trees can form the substantial upper story of a refuge. Although they have thorns, these are not like the bristling armor of many cactus plants. Although the branches make a solid roof, there is open space next to the ground. In that open space a hurrying desert animal can reach a haven, protected from a hawk or an eagle by the forbidding barrier overhead. In it a desert bird can find security. The branches overhead are a roof which is accessible from below but not from above.

Time after time, as we visited one or another part of the neighboring desert, we were almost sure to come upon a jackrabbit and to witness his swift departure. The flight of a jackrabbit is like a silent explosion. From his hidden retreat in the hollow of a clump of grass he has watched your approach, step by step. No slightest movement betrays his presence. Finally the instant arrives for action, and he is off and away. Even before you distinguish his form you are aware of swift motion. He is an expert in an instantaneous start.

If his course is over unencumbered ground, he wastes no time in needless bounds. His tall ears seem to follow a line that has no undulations, as if they were strung on a wire. If there are bushes in the way, he bounds over them, but no higher than necessary. Always he prefers territory that is relatively open, and shuns any that is too thickly covered. Within two or three seconds of his start he changes direction, and in another second or two he changes again.

By this time he is disappearing, and immediately he is no longer to be seen.

When they devised equipment for the jackrabbit they left nothing undone. His program was to win survival through flight — prompt, swift, and sure — not to rely on stealth or strategy, least of all on combat. Everything about him, from the tips of his ears to the ends of his toes, attests to the completeness of his preparation.

Since he must be able to detect any danger that may be approaching from any direction, his eyes must have full opportunity. So his skull is narrow and his eyes are elevated enough to command the whole horizon, right, left, front, and back, with only a slight movement of his head. His equipment for hearing is even more complete, since hearing can operate throughout the night when sight is not equally available. Those long ears have a reason. Their inner surface has but little hair, only enough to protect the skin. The ear is shaped to catch and amplify any sound. The two ears in combination can locate sound. Most of all, the ears can be rotated at the will of their owner. They are an efficient scanning device. His speed is beyond question. Those long hind legs can send him forward like a bullet. No other land animal can overtake him in the early moments of his getaway.

The food of a jack depends in part on the time of year. He is strictly a vegetarian. Therefore the spring rains

Jackrabbit

and the fall rains, with their quickened plant life, set his table with renewed bounty. They supply also the succulent foods that help to provide what water he needs. But he must live through the dry seasons as well, and to do this

he turns to the leaves on shrubs, especially mesquite. If he must have still more moisture, he sometimes secures it by nibbling the pads of prickly pear cactus. Somehow he makes a start at a pad by working between clusters of thorns, and then enlarges the entry. All through the dry season he conserves his own reserves of bodily moisture by avoiding the hot part of the day and doing his foraging in the evening and night.

That he is skillful in his use of food supplies is indicated by his strategic consumption of chili peppers. On some farms in the southern part of the desert, hot chilis are grown. When these are harvested and spread out to dry, the jacks come along at night and secure a succulent meal. Somehow they know that the hot part is especially present in the seeds. In the morning you will find little piles of seeds, all carefully discarded. The flesh of the pepper has been consumed, minus the offending contents.

A mystery of the desert rests on the brown and white form of another jack, called the antelope jackrabbit.

Like others of his clan, the antelope jack is a rangy, slender animal, who depends on a fast getaway and unbeatable speed for his safety when an enemy threatens. He is the unceasing objective of would-be captors, both on land and from the air. Coyotes are forever seeking to surprise him by stealthy approach, and to run fast enough to catch up with him if stealth fails. The coyotes themselves are fleet of foot, and the intended victim must be very fast in order to escape. Birds that live by hunting rival the coyote in their persistence. One of them, the caracara, is especially swift and is frequently on hand in the regions where the antelope jack is most at home.

Like others among the jackrabbits, the antelope jack has his resting place in a grassy region, a little hollow beneath a concealing bush. In his hollow he lies close to the ground, making no motion, but scanning the surrounding area for any least indication of approaching danger. His ears are very sensitive and are unbelievably tall. Their length is about one-third that of the owner's body. Since the food of the antelope jack is always herbage native to the desert, such as grass and the leaves of some desert shrubs, he must forage frequently and must have more than one resting place.

When an enemy approaches him as he lies in his hollow, he remains motionless until the very last split second of concealment and safety. Then, almost beneath the enemy's feet, he is off. With ears laid back on his neck and shoulders, he seems almost like something carried by the wind. He follows no straight course, but swiftly zigzags. This is where the mystery begins.

On his rump the antelope jack has a patch of long white hairs. Under ordinary conditions they are concealed by the bordering brown hairs. But they are controlled by muscles, and the jack can erect them. Also, muscles can move the skin that carries the bordering brown hairs, drawing them away.

The mystery continues. As the jack zigzags, changing

direction repeatedly, the white patch flashes up first on one side of the rump, then on the other. Seemingly the fleeing animal controls the location of the flash, and seemingly it appears on the side toward the pursuer. It might be conjectured that this only advertises the location of the animal at the instant of the flash. But it must be remembered that swift changes of direction are taking place, and the whole course of the pursuit is occupying only seconds. Perhaps the pursuer is baffled by the shifting objective, and the jack gains enough fractions of a second to make good his escape.

No one can say positively how the performance works. It remains another mystery of the desert.

Nearly always an animal that seeks the protection of a desert refuge is traveling at top speed to reach the haven. Often the animal may be a jackrabbit, and often the pursuer may be a coyote, the desert animal that can equal the speed of a jack and can maintain the speed for the essential length of time, perhaps for a longer time than the jack can command.

Although you may have spent many months in the desert Southwest, you may not have seen a coyote. Of one fact you may be sure, however. Although you have had no glimpse, the animals have seen you and have studied you as you went about doing whatever you had on hand to do.

This was our experience, until one day when we were driving slowly along a little-used desert road which is bordered by bushy country. Suddenly a jackrabbit crossed the road in front of us. He was running close to the ground, making maximum time. An instant later a gray streak crossed the road. In the half-second required for the crossing, there was no opportunity to observe details, but the animal was unquestionably a coyote. Like the jack he ran close to the ground. His color was an indiscriminate ashy, yellowish gray. His size was that of a small shepherd dog. In his swift course he was the personification of intense, determined pursuit.

By good fortune we could see from our car what happened next. On the farther side of the road, and a little way back from its margin, a clump of shrubs, bluish gray and three or four feet high, blocked the line of pursuit. The jack cleared them in one long bound and instantly continued his swift course across the desert, avoiding or clearing other clumps as he ran. The coyote made no attempt to bound over the clump near the road, but used up two or three seconds finding a way around. By the time this had been accomplished the jack had disappeared in the distance. Once more the fortresses of the desert had played their role as refuge.

If there is any one animal that illustrates better than any other the maximum of adaptability and resourcefulness, that animal may well be the coyote. In geographical range of territory, he is established all the way from the southern desert to the valleys of Alaska, although in the early settlement of this continent he claimed only the prairie states. In range of altitude, and the climate that goes with altitude, he inhabits successfully the low-lying desert country and the slopes that climb the mountains to the realm of evergreen forests and deep winter snows.

His food is as varied as his range of territory. Always he prefers freshly killed animal life, from gophers and kangaroo rats to rabbits and porcupines. But this is only the start. When that which he prefers is not available, almost anything else will do, including frogs, any fish that can be secured, dead or alive, any fruits that can be found, any vegetables, juniper seeds, mesquite beans, and grasshoppers if they chance to be handy. Since wild food may be scarce and domestic supplies available, his food may include poultry. When the territory that he adopts includes the range where sheep are pastured, and when lambing season is at hand, a newly born lamb that chances to be alone may be added to the diet.

In his search for food a coyote may range over many miles in the course of a single night. He is as nearly tireless as an animal can be. Starting from his home den in the afternoon or early evening, he may cover thirty or forty

Coyote

miles of rough territory by the time of his return. The den is seldom one that has been deliberately constructed by its occupant. There are too many suitable places already available, such as a fox burrow that can be enlarged, a badger home in acceptable ground, a hollow under the shelter of a hillside bush that is strategically located, a cavity in the midst of tumbled rocks.

Wherever it may be, a den is shared by a coyote and his mate during the coming of a new generation. Although it is not furnished with any bedding material, it has the advantage that it can be kept clean. Usually the new arrivals will number seven or eight. After they are weaned, and until they are on their own, the father helps to keep them supplied with food. When this period is over, each one must find his own place and live his own life.

Strange as it may seem, a young coyote, before his wilderness ways are established, can become tame and trusting, not at all like some other animals. He seems to have no inherent antipathy toward human beings.

Understandably the coyote, with his sagacity, plays a part in the legends of some American Indian tribes, who felt that they saw in him some human traits. An Aztec word, *coyot'l,* is the source of the name "coyote."

The Peaceful

At the same hour every evening, when the last trace of lingering daylight has faded from the sky, a furry animal silently appears outside our kitchen window. He has come for the supper, whatever it may be, that has been spread for him on the broad top of a stump, a few feet from the house. Thoroughly and silently he searches for every crumb. Since there are cracks and cavities in the top of the stump, he explores these minutely, without any hurry or carelessness. If some other animal approaches, he does not snarl or utter any protesting sound. When the last morsel has been recovered, he quietly leaves the stump and disappears in the gathering darkness.

He is the gray fox of the Southwest country, a cousin of the red fox of the East, but as unlike that familiar animal as if they were members if a different race. The red is crafty and tricky. His wits have been sharpened in his long contact with men and dogs. When he is pursued he knows how to throw both the men and the dogs off the track. When a trap

Gray Fox

is set for him he knows how to avoid it. When a poultry house has been left unguarded, he knows how to contrive entrance and to carry off one of the occupants. He is an able member of a sophisticated world.

The gray is an accomplished animal of the outdoor wilderness, graceful, alert, with sharp eyes, keen ears, and responsive muscles. His food is the small animal life of the desert, which he prefers to capture alive. Since the desert is rich in mice and ground squirrels, gophers and pack rats, lizards and sometimes the smaller rabbits, these are the greater part of his daily fare. Since these creatures are abroad in the dusk of evening and in the darkness of night, the fox also is out on his hunting trips in these same hours. Since his objectives are active and alert, he must be equally fast and sure.

Since the gray fox is fond of fruits and nuts, he supplements his diet with these added finds. When he runs across small birds that rest on the ground, he welcomes them. When there would be an advantage in an approach from some spot above ground, he climbs a tree. Always he is a master of ambush, and he is willing to stand motionless for a long period while awaiting the right moment to pounce.

His den is in some sheltered and hidden place in the midst of rocks, or in a hollow in the earth, or in a convenient log. During the heat of midsummer he is likely to move to a higher and cooler region. In the fall he reverses his journey. Wherever he may be, he is a well-groomed citizen of the desert country, with large and attentive ears, and a bushy tail tipped with black.

Far to the south an area of smooth desert sand is marked with many small footprints. They are shallow prints, as round as a coin. They look as if they might have been made by someone's pet cat. The animal that made the print is, in fact, not much larger than a domestic cat, and is equally soft and fluffy. If the observer could be on hand in the hours of early night, or perhaps when night is changing to dawn, he might see the smallest known member of the fox clan, the kit fox.

He would find it a gentle creature, full of curiosity, not easily frightened. Its fur is dense and almost white, a protective whiteness against a background of light sand. A slight shade of gray is added by some scattered longer hairs which are tipped with black. The ears are large and covered with fur, inside and out; they denote the keen sense of hearing that their owner possesses. The legs are rather short, and the feet are well covered with hair, useful when walking silently on sand. The tail is long and fluffy, and at the very end is tipped with black.

The animal will be alone, as is his way. He is out on his accustomed foraging trip, in search of small animal life, especially the kangaroo rats that are abundant in his region. Capturing one of these shows his quickness and dexterity. Whatever the prize may be, he carries it home to eat.

Home is a burrow, usually one which belonged originally to a ground squirrel and has been enlarged by the new owner. Deep in the burrow the present occupant, with his mate, finds security. In this shelter the young are born, and in this home the father of the litter assumes his full share of duties, foraging for the youngsters until they can fend for themselves. In all this the kit fox shares existence with a mate to whom he remains attached for life.

Almost every day a graceful, appealing animal crossed an open space near our house. Sometimes there were two or three, traveling together. Once there was a very small member of the group, following in the footsteps of a full-grown male and followed by a guardian, perhaps the young-ster's mother. Small and clean cut hoof marks in the sandy floor of a nearby canyon were signatures. The space between the two hooves was narrow. The imprint was pointed. The visitors were whitetail deer.

In the southeastern part of the desert country there are many whitetail. The various groups of mountains, rising from a base that may be three-thousand feet or more above sea level, and reaching a height of six-thousand feet or more, provide regions with characteristics that the whitetail find agreeable. In the canyons there are gradations of climate and vegetation. In the open valleys, where canyons give way to terraces and level spaces, there are further variations.

In the mid-winter months the deer are likely to resort to the lower regions, especially in mountains that are high enough to accumulate snow. At lower altitudes they can avoid the hampering snowfall and can find available browse for food. With warm weather a reverse movement is in order. Browse in higher regions becomes attractive, and a suitable place for the advent of fawns is available. At the same time, the nuisance of flies and other insects is diminished.

Wherever it may be seen, a whitetail is an appealing animal. Its body is smoothly formed and pleasingly clad. Its legs taper to slenderness. If it is startled and runs away, its small tail, which provides the reason for its name, is much in evidence. At rest the tail is held snugly against the body and shows only dark-colored hairs. But the moment the owner is startled and begins to run, the tail is elevated,

Whitetail Deer

straight up. The underside is pure white, and so are the hairs that lie beneath it. Instantly the tail is waved repeatedly from side to side, like a signal flag. The gait of the fleeing animal is fast, but the deer does not rise in high bounds. To make sure its escape, it zigzags.

Historically, the whitetail deer has played an appealing part. It was the source of the buckskin used for clothing by pioneers in the East and by early settlers in the West. In regions farther north, and in rugged country across the continent, it still supplies the materials for many articles, from gloves to moccasins.

Wherever it may be found, from the Rockies to the Southwest desert, to run across a whitetail is an event, and to find its tracks in the sand of a desert canyon is an invitation to a further meeting.

The mule deer is like a large cousin of the whitetail deer, a cousin who carries an imposing set of antlers, and who likes to travel with several of his kind. The whitetail

Mule Deer

Pronghorn Antelope

favors the eastern part of the deer country, while the mule deer favors the western part.

Two animals that you can see and enjoy in the Southwest country, the pronghorn antelope and the prairie dog, share a similar experience, though in different degree. For each one, home territory was once the vast area of grassland that extended from the Rockies hundreds of miles to the east. For each the coming of farmland and cattle ranges meant acceptance of increased restrictions, and this in turn meant diminished numbers. In the Southwest today and in bordering areas both may be seen, the antelope especially in more extensive country.

The great numbers of pronghorn antelopes that once prevailed are well pictured in the journals of Lewis and Clark. In 1804, the explorers, encamped on the Missouri River, wrote in their journal, "vast herds of Buffalo, Deer,

Elk, and Antelopes were seen feeding in every direction as far as the eye of the observer could reach." Soon afterward, Lewis, who had tried to approach a small band of antelope, wrote of "the rapidity of their flight along a ridge . . . It appeared rather the rapid flight of birds than the motion of quadrupeds. I think I can safely venture the assertion that the speed of this animal is equal if not superior to that of the finest blooded courser."

In modern times the speed of the antelope has been tested by various observers. The fact is well established that the animal, when at its best and when hard pressed, can attain a speed of a mile a minute for a limited distance. It can run at forty miles an hour for several miles. It is indeed fleet footed, and in its performance it is graceful and attractive as well as unbelievably fast.

The antelope is not a large animal. Although it is easily seen on the open range that it prefers, it is somewhat smaller than a whitetail deer. Its general color is dark tan above and white beneath. Two white bands are seen on the under side of its neck, and there are black markings on its face. Especially conspicuous, as the animal runs away, is its rump patch of long white hairs, which it can erect at will.

Its horns do not branch repeatedly, as do those of a deer or an elk, and they are not shed completely at the end of a growing period. A solid core remains, attached to the skull. A curving, sharp-pointed horn grows on and around this core. A broad and blunt extension is attached to the horn near the base.

In its former great expanse of territory, the antelope was a grazing animal. Native grasses were its preferred food, but the pressure of advancing farm land brought about adaptations. Gradually the antelope was obliged to abandon the rich lands that Lewis and Clark wrote about, and to retreat to higher altitudes. Grazing continued where possible, but other plants, such as rabbitbrush, were utilized, and to some extent the animals accepted the leaves on shrubs.

In their retreat to higher altitudes they stopped short of any reliance on mountain regions that would be buried in snow for prolonged periods. A summertime journey into such a region would be followed by a return to lower country. An antelope is not an animal of deep snows.

Visit, sometime, a place in the grassland region of the Southwest where prairie dogs are established. What you will see, will follow the characteristic pattern of any prairie dog community anywhere.

One end of a long area is dotted with scattered low mounds, perhaps a dozen of them. Pasture grass, six inches high, covers the area, except around the mounds where it is clipped short. Each mound has a depression in the top. In the center of the depression there is a hole, a few inches in diameter. The earth around the hole and over the rest of the mound is bare and is packed down firmly. In a way, a mound is like a circular dike around a hole. No occupants of the holes are in sight. If the place is a community, it seems deserted.

A few minutes later, earth begins to fly up from one of the holes. It comes in spurts, and goes far enough to clear the dike around the hole. Evidently the occupant is enlarging his premises. He is not following the plan of carrying the earth out, as would a chipmunk, but is kicking it out with his hind feet and legs. Presently the spurts of earth stop and a small round head appears. After a few moments the owner climbs out and sits upright on the rim around the hole.

He is a plump, smooth-coated, brownish animal and looks well fed. Sitting straight up he is about twelve inches tall. His legs are short, the hind pair serving to give him a secure upright position. His demeanor is one of friendliness and curiosity. At the same time he is watchful of his surroundings, making sure that no hawk or eagle is overhead, and that no fox or coyote is crouching in the grass beyond the clipped area.

In a few minutes other heads appear at the openings of other holes, and other plump forms are sitting up on earth dikes. A small chatter begins. Presently one of the mound-owners leaves his lookout post, moves out through the clipped surroundings, and begins to nibble the longer grass. Others follow, here and there, each in his own direction. The mounds are almost deserted, but not quite. One sentry remains on duty, alert and watchful. A few minutes later something happens. Perhaps a hawk wings into sight, or the tall grass in the distance is stirred by the movement of a coyote, crouching close to the ground. Instantly the sentry lets out a sharp yipping bark and follows it with a rapid succession of other high-pitched barks. Without waiting an instant, his fellow-townsmen run full-tilt for their mounds and dive into their holes. As the last prairie dog disappears, the sentry also makes his dive, and the mounds are empty.

For several minutes nothing is heard or seen. Then in the hollow at the top of one mound a brown head appears, raised just enough to permit its owner's eyes to scan the surroundings over the earth rim. Gradually other owners do the same. After a further interval a smooth, brown body appears, upright on the earth of a rim. No alarm follows. In half a minute the incident is over, the mounds are occupied, and a vigorous chatter begins, continuing until the owners of mounds once more scatter out to resume feeding.

The quarters below a mound follow a well-established plan. A few inches below the opening there is an offset, like a shelf or a partial room. This is the place where the owner waits while he listens for the sound of any approaching enemy. It is like the peephole in a locked front door. The owner can survey the situation without himself being seen and without undue risk. The place is advantageous for listening. A position farther down in the tunnel would unquestionably be safe, but would be too remote to be of practical use, as if the owner of a house with a locked front door were obliged to depend on the kitchen window instead of the peephole.

Below this listening point the tunnel narrows to a diameter equal to that of the owner but not big enough for a larger animal. The tunnel soon turns here and there, and branches. At the end of one branch it enlarges to form a chamber, which may be eight or ten inches in diameter and equipped with dried grasses or other vegetation for a mattress and for warmth. There is no storage place for food.

Unlike a chipmunk, the prairie dog does not lay up supplies to be used through mid-winter. He eats abundantly in the fall, accumulates a reserve of fat, and draws on that to carry him through until a new season has brought about new green forage. All through the rainy months his well-tramped dike around the opening to his quarters is his protection against floods. The region where he lives may be covered with three inches of standing water, but his home remains dry.

A big boulder, as large as a small house, rests in the middle of a broad terrace near a cottage where we spent many weeks. An evergreen oak with spreading branches keeps it company. Smaller boulders lie nearby, with mesquite trees and small bushes in their midst.

Every morning, after the sun is well up, a small dark animal, the size of an extra-large gray squirrel, appears on the big boulder and settles down in a chosen spot from which he can view the surroundings. Although a limb of the oak is overhead and would extend the view, the animal never climbs up there. The boulder is his choice. He is a furry animal, gray on his foreparts, then darker, with distinct bands. His bushy tail, nearly as long as his body, shows prominent bands. If you watch him from a distance and stand motionless, he gives no sign of awareness of your presence; but when you move an arm, even slightly, he leaves his big boulder instantly and disappears somewhere at its base, signaling his departure with a quavering whistle.

Appropriately the shy visitor is called a rock squirrel. Although he has the build of a gray squirrel, his ways are completely different. He can climb a tree if he chooses, or jump from one limb to another, but he usually has no desire to do so. He is not arboreal. Neither is he terrestrial, in the sense of liking to be on the ground. He does not burrow and occupy a tunnel in the earth, in the manner of ground squirrels. His choice is a big boulder, wherever that can be found, and he likes bushes and trees near at hand for protection against hawks and other enemies. His preferred private apartment is a narrow, winding space in the midst of rocks. This is his home when a family is on the way. This also is his retreat in stormy weather.

He is a daytime animal, not a night-time wanderer. His food includes almost everything that the desert country makes available — juniper berries, seeds, acorns, cactus fruits, mesquite beans, roots and tubers, anything that is obtainable through daylight hours. When the appropriate season arrives he climbs the tall stalk of a century plant to secure the seeds. This kind of climbing seems to be different from climbing trees.

As summer moves along, the rock squirrel lays up supplies of food for winter use. His storehouse is multiple. His own private quarters are used, but various cavities in the midst of the rocks serve as additional receptacles. Always he lives his own life, never as a member of a community in which stores and quarters are shared.

The Southwest is home territory. He is not a dweller in the North and East. Perhaps only the Southwest can provide for him the right kind of big boulders, with a suitable combination of adjacent trees and bushes and acceptable open ground.

The stump to which the silent gray fox comes at dusk each evening has a tree growing closely beside it, a sprawling young sycamore, about as tall as the house. Up there in the tree food is attached to a limb. Everything is as fully in view from the kitchen window as the broad top of the stump where the fox has supper. Up there, sometime in the night, another silent visitor pays a call. Unlike a raccoon, to which he is related, he leaves no track, no imprint of knobby fingers, for his paws are soft and furry. He does not come when anyone is stirring, or when a light is shining. Unlike a coati, who is equally good at climbing but likes the company of companions, the shy stranger comes alone. Nothing is disarranged, but the food is consumed.

If you can catch sight of him, you find that he is a gentle and appealing creature, with a wistful face and great brown eyes. Although he is related to a family that makes no secret of its presence, this quiet member is seldom seen in public. His name also is simple and not distinguished, for he is known as a ringtail cat.

Faithful to family traditions, he has a banded tail. It is a handsome tail, soft and fluffy and as long as its owner's body. He is not the grizzled warrior that a raccoon is likely to be, but is soft and gentle. Although he is nearly as long as a raccoon, he weighs no more than a quarter as much. Across his face he has a sketchy reminder of a mask, but with a broad white band around each eye. His legs are rather short. His feet leave a round track, and his toes bear only the necessary claws for climbing.

Sometimes the ringtail's home is in the traditional hollow tree, but usually it is in some horizontal cleft in the

Ringtail

rocks of a cliff, or in a canyon wall. This is his preferred resting place through daylight hours. When darkness settles down and gives him protection, he starts out on his search for food. He prefers small animal life, but welcomes fruits and larger insects. In his foraging he is as much at home in trees as on the ground. Before daylight returns, he has retired to the seclusion and safety of his retreat in a rock wall.

The human visitor in the desert country may find the ringtail's track, small and round, like that of a domestic cat. The clue to the animal's identity becomes more probable if his work is in evidence. It becomes positive if the visitor chances to spend a few nights in a desert cabin where mice are numerous. All at once in a single night, there are no more mice. In the dust or sand outdoors, there are small round footprints. There has been no telltale sound in the night, and there is no revealing glimpse in the morning, but a ringtail has had a rewarding visit. Events like this are the reason why, in earlier periods, when mining was widely under way in desert mountains, the ringtail acquired another name, the miner's cat.

The Unpredictable

As we have traveled here and there in the Southwest desert country, we have reached a firm conclusion about the desert. Our conclusion is not derogatory. It simply is firm. It runs as follows. There is only one fact about the desert that is completely certain, and that fact is that no such absolute certainty exists. There may be only one chance in a million that something specific is going to take place, but somehow eventually that remote chance becomes reality. The desert is definitely unpredictable. This fact is one aspect of its rich interest.

We had long been familiar with the raccoon in the wooded country of the East and the North, and we had supposed that the desert would have its own version of the animal, as it has with various others. The desert itself has its own characteristics, and these would logically be reflected in adaptations of its animal life. Vast spaces where bushes grow, but no sizeable trees, would seem far removed from the forests that are home to the well-known animal that wears a black mask and leads dogs a noisy chase while on his way to his home in a tree, or while making a detour in order to walk through a stream and thereby throw pursuers off the track.

But the desert country of the Southwest includes territory that is not exclusively characterized by sand and treeless plains. There are mountains, and in them are valleys that descend from wooded heights. In some valleys a stream flows during part of the year, and along the border of the stream are big trees. This is raccoon territory, with food in the stream and on the banks, and with acceptable shelter in piles of rocks or in caves, as desirable as a hollow in a tree and probably a safer haven.

In the desert, as in other regions, the raccoon himself supplies other essentials. In the desert valleys, as in the forests of the East or North, he is clever and resourceful. He can run rapidly if need be. He can climb a tree readily and dispose himself comfortably in a fork high above the ground. He can wade a stream wherever one is available, and can swim if necessity arises. He can fight an enemy and inflict heavy punishment. He can thrive on the food obtainable from the desert and the canyon.

A raccoon's feet need no special adaptation. They are remarkable as they are. As he crosses moist sand he leaves a track that points to the story. Both front feet and hind feet have long toes with knobby joints and useful claws. With his front feet he can do whatever serves his needs and desires. With these capable substitutes for hands he secures and manipulates his food.

In the stream that flows in the bed of the canyon, and in the pool where it ends as it leaves the canyon, there are mussels and crayfish, frogs and perhaps small fish. Those creatures that are slow-moving are brought out by the raccoon onto the bank, and those that are active may be caught. The capable front feet of the raccoon search the bottom of any stream and explore the hidden hollows under the banks. Mussels are opened, and the empty shells discarded. Frog legs are neatly skinned. Usually, if water is available, a raccoon likes to immerse his food and rub it with his front feet before he eats it.

When the right season has arrived, food is obtained from sources that are not near a canyon and its occasional stream. Wild berries are sought, and the acorns from oak trees, but especially the beans on mesquite trees, often abundant. If moist ground happens to be near, where earthworms are present, the forager discovers them and digs up as many as possible. If desirable food requires that the raccoon climb the brushy bank of a canyon, his capable front feet again play a part. They can grasp a bush and help to pull him up a steep slope.

In all of these activities, the owner of the mask and the clever hands is only occasionally seen. He begins his rounds when dusk has immersed the desert, and he is safely back home before sunrise. Only his tracks and the results of his foraging remain to disclose his adventures.

In the spring of the year and again in the fall, he changes his clothes, wearing a lighter weight fur garment in summer, and a warmer coat in the fall. But always in the desert or in far distant forests, he wears his black mask. Always he has a bushy tail with alternating light and dark bands. Always he likes to have water within reasonable reach. And always, if you chance to see him face to face, you agree that his pointed nose and his well-set eyes bespeak an animal whose native cleverness is unsurpassed by most other dwellers in the desert.

In the midst of the specialized inhabitants of the desert country, the familiar porcupine pursues his standard, time-honored way. Other animals may have developed habits and characteristics that enable them to survive in the desert. The porcupine survives with the same equipment and procedures that his clan everywhere have found useful for untold centuries.

In canyons of the desert country, trees grow that serve the porcupine's needs. In winter he can climb a suitable tree, rest comfortably in a crotch, and enjoy the nearby inner bark that provides for him a nutritious meal. In the canyon's mouth and out in the open, some trees carry clusters of mistletoe. These are a special delicacy. When poplars and willows are coming into leaf, their catkins are an addition to the porcupine's diet. In summer, the leaves on acceptable shrubs, and the stalks and leaves of various smaller plants, continue the desert's offering. An antler lying on the desert floor, or a bone of any kind, offers variety and perhaps a desirable addition to diet. When one is found by the porcupine, it is thoroughly gnawed.

On the ground a porcupine is a temptation to a larger animal — a bobcat or a mountain lion. He cannot run from danger. His legs are too short, his body too heavy, and his gait too slow. He can and will resort to a time-tested procedure. Arching his back and tucking his head down between his forelegs, he elevates his armament of sharp quills, holds his punishing tail in readiness, and awaits events. If the threatening animal is wise, there is no attack. If caution does not prevail, a face full of quills is in order. The quills are thoroughly barbed along the outer end, and the barbs point backward toward the base. In addition, it appears that the barbs on a quill which is buried in warm flesh move outward away from the body of the quill, thus anchoring it in its position.

The den of a porcupine is in some rocky shelter, such as a small cave in the wall of a canyon. In this retreat a porcupine pair have their one offspring. There is only one each year. They have none of the margin of safety enjoyed by animals that have two or more young, or perhaps more than one generation a year. The fact that the porcupine clan continues to hold its own throughout the vast territory that it inhabits, tells the story of ancestral ways that were successful and have been explicitly followed.

Sometimes a woodsman chances to acquire a baby porcupine and discovers that the animal, in friendly hands, is gentle. Treated as a pet, it does not raise its quills, offers no threat, and responds to kindess as would a household pet. In the forest it is slow moving, but it is not by nature slow witted.

Following a road that bordered a steep mountain flank, we came upon a band of ten or twelve wild turkeys. They were crossing the road and climbing the steep slope on its other side, in the midst of out-thrust ledges, tangled bushes, and stunted trees. They seemed not in the least alarmed by our coming, but steadily proceeded with their climb, picking their way around obstacles, sometimes each one for himself, sometimes three or four following a leader. They were like the turkeys on an eastern farm when the hour has come to retire to roosts in trees.

As a matter of fact they were the counterparts of domestic turkeys, although living in the desert country. They had the same compact body, clad in closely fitting feathers, the same strong legs, and the same long neck that could give a wide view of surroundings and could detect dangers. An inconspicuous variant in their dress, a slightly different marking, would identify them, but in other aspects they were the same as farm turkeys anywhere. Once more the desert was unpredictable in its ways, using the familiar and requiring nothing new.

The band of turkeys crossing the road was on its way from an open space below the road, where there were a few broken-down apple trees, the survivors of a former orchard. Apparently the turkeys were returning to a ridge above the steep flank. Dusk was approaching, and it was time to seek tree limbs on which to roost. The band seemed to be following a schedule, leaving their haven at daybreak and returning to it at dusk. Any outlying farm in the East could provide a parallel.

A few days later we returned to the same spot, but the band was nowhere to be seen. Since the hour was late in the afternoon, it seemed likely that they had left the place and returned to the top of the ridge. But in the abandoned orchard a big turkey still remained, like a straggler who was not yet ready to turn in for the night. Diligently he was exploring the ground under one of the trees, scratching vigorously with his strong legs and armored claws, sending bunches of grass and clods of earth flying behind him. Presently he moved to another tree and then another. But dusk was closing in. Even while we watched, he silently disappeared.

Everywhere you travel in the desert country you are continually reminded of the specialized measures that protect the leaves of plants, and the flowers and fruits, from consumption by hungry animals. There seems to be no end to the thorns, large and small, that guard approach by a foraging visitor.

But the story is not complete. Having accomplished its program of defense, the desert seems sometimes to adopt an unexpected course. On the mountain slopes, on the terraces where canyons give way to lower ground, a shrub grows, the jojoba, which often is called the goatnut or deernut, or sometimes the coffeeberry. Usually it is three or four feet high, sometimes five. Its leaves are smooth and firm, neither crowded nor thinly arranged. Their color is gray-green, and they continue their modest display all through winter. When warm weather arrives, the plant bears inconspicuous blossoms. These are followed by a nut that looks somewhat like a long acorn.

These attractions are not overlooked by visitors. The leaves are sought by deer, who find them an acceptable addition to available food supplies. The nuts are harvested and stored by ground squirrels. Human beings also enter the picture. Although the nuts have a flavor that to the white man seems bitter, Indians have turned them to good account. When the kernel is dried and roasted, it has served as a coffee substitute. Also the dried kernel may be ground to a powder, sugar added, and the combination made up into candy.

To these facts it seems that the desert gives no heed. There are no thorns on the trunk or limbs of the plant, no

Wild Turkey

spines on leaf or nut. The deer can browse all they wish, and the squirrels are at liberty to carry off the acorn-like nuts. There is no barrier of any kind around the shrub.

The desert is unpredictable.

Sometimes it seems that circumstances deprive the desert of any opportunity to be unpredictable. Conditions do not lend themselves to an unexpected turn of events.

Wherever you go in the Southwest desert country you are likely to see trees that carry clusters of mistletoe on their branches. Sometimes a tree is heavily loaded and shows the effect of its invaders. The tribe of mistletoe is an extensive one, with many members. Although they may differ, one from another, all of them have one similarity in their manner of existence. Sometime in the remote past an ancestor of the mistletoe must have learned to live at the expense of other plants. In the course of untold ages the plan became the accepted way of life.

Strangely, a mistletoe is a complete plant, with leaves that may be inconspicuous but that nevertheless are foliage, and with flowers that become fertilized and produce seeds. The berries, sometimes conspicuous, are the containers for the seeds. But here the self-sufficiency of the plant comes to an end. It must of course have moisture and food supplies. It does not obtain these on its own, but secures them from the tree or shrub to which it is attached.

The start of the attachment to a host lies in the seed. The berry that accompanies the seed is relished by birds. In fact, the berries of some kinds of mistletoe are a prime source of food for several familiar birds, and a source of moisture for birds in regions of scanty rainfall. The host tree, with roots deep in the ground, is able to secure moisture which birds could not obtain.

When the berries are carried off by birds, the seeds, which are sticky, are transported to the twigs of trees. Thus the stage is set for a new mistletoe plant in a new location. At this point a curious situation may develop. Although a seed may be gummy and may easily stick to a twig, and although it may germinate, the new mistletoe plant may not be able to gain a foothold. Seemingly, the tree may decline to be a host. For example, the ironwood of the Southwest has been observed to exude a gummy substance at the point where the invading young mistletoe is about to make a start. This substance engulfs the invader, then hardens, and presently falls to the ground.

Of all the mistletoe seeds and all the berries, only a few succeed in growing, but these are enough to maintain the mistletoe population.

The unpredictable nature of the desert is accompanied by some developments that are not at all distressing but are amusing.

Wherever you may go, and wherever the land and its surroundings are suitable, you see the narrow-leaf yucca, sometimes a dozen or two in a broad open space, sometimes a few crowded together in a small pocket, sometimes a hundred or more scattered far and wide. Always you are tempted to the conclusion that the narrow-leaf yucca must have a hidden weakness in its character, which inclines it toward irresponsible behavior.

Following the accepted, orthodox pattern, it begins its career as a clump of sharp-pointed, narrow leaves, close to the ground. From time to time, season to season, the clump is enlarged upward by the addition of more leaves at the top. Thus it slowly develops a central core, like a tree trunk. In this way the plant gradually acquires height. While this process is going on, the lowest leaves lose their activity and their green color. Having no further function to perform, they cease to extend their length outward and upward, but turn downward and lie flat against the central core, as if they were the shaggy bark on the trunk of a tree.

Sometimes in the course of this process, perhaps early, perhaps at a later period, the yucca embarks on a blossoming career. From the top of the trunk a flower stalk shoots up, sends out short branches near its top, and displays heavy blossoms. When the blossoms have concluded their career, woody containers take their place and seeds are ready. In due time, as the seasons move along, the plant is ready for another blossoming adventure, and again a flower stalk is developed, with its load of heavy blossoms.

All this is orthodox. But the narrow-leaf yucca is prone to variations from the standard plan. As you cross a wide expanse, where scores of the plants are in view, you see numerous examples of the unorthodox. It looks as if certain plants had not studied the rules. Other kinds of plants seem to have a definite pattern. A given tree, for example, branches as it should and attains a prescribed form. In fact some trees can be identified by their form without examination of details. A narrow-leaf yucca would have to be named by its lack of conformity.

Uncertainty begins with the trunk, when it is still only a few inches tall. The plant may develop a fork and thus have two trunks from a single base. As growth proceeds, the two trunks may become three, and the three may become four. Observation of a large expanse of yuccas will reveal examples.

If a plant adheres to a single trunk, and if it attains considerable height, the task of maintaining a straight, perpendicular form seems to grow difficult. A curved trunk is frequent. If there are two or three trunks from a common base, the result may be fantastic.

The story of the flower stalk adds to the uncertainty. Presumably it should rise straight from the top of the trunk. Often it does so, but often it starts off at an angle. Often three or four flower stalks will rise from a single crown.

All of this means a confused array as you look across an expanse in which many yuccas are growing. But it also means that this is the way of the narrow-leaf yucca, which somehow has become one of the desert's irresponsibles.

As if to add to the desert's uncertainty, tumbleweeds arrive on the scene. When you visit land that lies in level benches, preferably land that is irrigated, you are seeing the preferred home of tumbleweeds. The broad area will have the moisture that the newcomer likes. When a crop has been harvested and the land is ready for an invader, tumbleweeds have a situation to their liking. In addition, the border of a field, next to the fence, is equally inviting and unoccupied. Then comes the stage in which fully grown tumbleweeds, detached from the ground and rolling along, as is their way, are able to play their full part in enactment of an unscheduled desert show.

When it has room, the individual tumbleweed tends to take on a globular shape. It may not fully achieve this, but at least it will have a rounded contour and can roll. Sometimes a plant will be a well-rounded ball five feet or more in diameter. Its structure is firm and its surface rigid. It is attached to the ground in such way that it can break loose when it is mature and dry. It does not build up a low mound beneath it, as do some other desert plants when the wind blows and sand grains are on the move. The surface of the ground beneath it remains smooth and level. In time the plant loses its anchorage, and with the wind sweeping it along, it embarks on its travels.

A crowd of tumbleweeds that have rolled across a field and arrived at a fence or a highway are a helpless lot. They make you feel that someone must have given them misinformation or bad advice, and that because of this they are now at a loss what to do. Little and big alike, they are baffled and in trouble, but the bigger the subject the more baffling the problem. A little tumbleweed, no larger than a football, can roll between the wheels of a passing car, but a big one must take the chance of being run over.

In unoccupied country subsequent events may not be exciting. But fences and highways, and even railway tracks, get into the picture. Behind a fence the travelers congregate until the long pile of them is as high as the fence itself. A great brown ball, three or four feet in diameter, crossing a highway, startles an approaching motorist and makes him feel that he must swerve his car or come to a stop. An elongated ball coming down a village street, turning over and over like a gymnast, is almost humanly ludicrous. An agile ball, hurrying along a railway track ahead of a train, makes you feel that someone ought to flag the train or rescue the fugitive.

A tumbleweed is a confirmed adventurer in the outdoor world.

Desert Showcase

Within a few steps of the house that we have occupied through midwinter months, a mixed company fills the level space where a rocky gully leaves the mountain's flank. When winter is drawing to a close and spring has not yet fully arrived, the level area is a rough blend of the gray of leaf-less shrubs and the pale yellow of dead grass. In the midst of these, a joint fir raises stems that look like reeds and simulate from a distance a leafy bush. Where a low ledge enters the area, a prickly pear cactus holds fast to its spine-armored pads. In a corner of the opening, a narrow-leaf yucca, shoulder high, bears aloft a dead flower-stalk, half prostrate under the pressure of winter winds.

Although the open space is a terrace, rising higher than broad flats of creosote bushes down below, although it commands a mountain panorama, it offers sparing invitation. In its suspended life, the ashes of winter concealing the promise of spring, it is like the gray of a cloud-filled morning, the chill of a springtime overdue.

But within the mouth of the gully a transformation has been taking place, a promise is already fulfilled. A shrub, chest high, spreads curving limbs. Trunk and branches, which had borne a slight gray covering, now stand revealed in their own strong bark, a permanent garment that is rich mahogany red. Evergreen leaves, narrowly oval, clothe the twigs. As if to point always to the sun in the blue sky, each is borne on a stem which can twist, assuring that the leaf stand upright. As if to make certain that the sunlight will be reflected and directed all around, the surface of each leaf is lacquered.

Within the setting of the green leaves rests the plant's guarantee that spring is even now arriving. Little clusters of tiny flower buds, as rosy as a spring dawn, shelter in their midst other clusters which are like advance messengers of summer. With them each blossom is already fully formed, a little white vase with narrow neck and frilled opening. Thus the promise of a new season is set forth. The shrub that is the bearer of the message is a member of an illustrious clan, a cousin of the rhododendron.

Near the mountain's summit, and on other mountain heights across the continent, another member, the kinnikinnick, is preparing to announce the ending of winter. Its low trailing branches, hugging the rock, carry the small round fruits which have given it another familiar name, the bearberry.

The desert shrub, with the mahogany red bark and the lacquered leaves, also bears small round fruits. It was the Spanish tongue that gave this shrub its name, the Spanish word for "little apple," the manzanita.

The Arizona vireo, when it chooses a suitable situation for its nest, likes a place that to human eyes seems unkempt. If the surroundings offer a small stream or a pond, and if willows grow there, an open thicket will be inviting. If mesquites are present, making the place a somewhat thorny tangle, the invitation may be increased, although nothing as thorny as catclaws may be present.

Arizona Vireo

In this inviting thicket the vireo chooses a stalk of willow or mesquite, perhaps one with a fork near one end, and from this suspends a nest like a cup. Grass fibers are the materials used in weaving the cup, and in suspending it from the stalk. Sometimes a shredded leaf is added. In any case the nest is secure, and the unkempt thicket, with occasional thorns gives protection. The inconspicuous plumage of the bird increases its security. Its voice also is not arresting and revealing.

The Arizona vireo occupies extensive territory, including suitable locations from the central states to parts of the west coast and into Mexico.

Every spring the coming of rain in the desert country is the signal for a miracle. Sometimes the miracle is enacted in only small and scattered areas, perhaps too few and too small to be widely noted. Sometimes a certain region of the desert witnesses the spectacle, while others must wait until another year. Sometimes the stage is long and wide, and vast reaches of the desert take part.

Whether the drama be small or great, the desert sand is a principal actor. Upon that sand one or another of the desert's flowering plants, that bloom and then die, has dropped countless seeds. This may have taken place only a year ago, or five years, or ten. The seeds have the vitality to live on and on, if they can be in a medium in which they are protected from harm. They must not blow away, or be washed down to an unfriendly environment. They must be persuaded not to germinate too soon or too late. They must not be subjected to the attack of harmful organisms when the time comes for germination and growth.

The desert sand provides the medium in which the prolonged waiting can safely take place. Its very dryness is an essential quality. It is a storage chamber, which holds and protects the seeds entrusted to its care. If it were rich soil, it would harbor small organisms. The soil's fertility would in itself favor the large perennial plants, and these would be a handicap. Since the sand lies on level areas, or those which are gently sloping, it does not invite transport to gullies and washes. When the rains come, the droplets can penetrate through the midst of the sand grains.

In their penetration the drops find the seeds, and thus the other actors of the drama come upon the stage along with the sand. If the rain is brief, nothing can take place, and the drama cannot be completed. If the rain falls upon a rocky slope but misses the gentle area, the drama cannot be started. But here and there in the desert, the seeds lie waiting, and here and there the rains come and continue. Almost overnight, slopes and plains that were dull or bare become flower gardens, as richly colored as a great painting.

The unassuming sand has fulfilled its mission.

It would seem that sometime in the remote past, a member of the poppy clan found an acceptable vacant area somewhere in the desert and began to grow there. Its plants were only six or eight inches tall, but each of them branched near the base and sent up several flower stems. Each stem carried a papery blossom, and when the blossom had faded, it was followed by a supply of seeds, which dropped into crevices of sand. In the course of time more and more plants occupied desert areas that had been vacant, and more seeds found a resting place in the sand.

Thus the stage was prepared for a pageant that has been enacted from time to time through the years since the clan moved into the waiting area, a move that was duplicated in scores of other similar areas. So it has come about that a great robe of gold is spread over parts of the desert in years when the rain comes in large enough amounts to quicken the seeds in the sand.

In countless gardens across the country a cousin of the desert poppy opens its golden blossoms. So it happens also that a state which borders the desert and shares in a part of it chooses a golden member of the poppy clan as state flower.

In another and different way the clan established a place in the desert country. A poppy that grows to be eighteen inches tall or more is widely distributed in various regions, often taking over ground that is stony or alkaline or both. When we visited a region in the southern part of the desert country, the tall poppies kept us company. Far to the north, in a different region, they occupied the roadside border. Their papery blossom is white, and may be more than two inches broad. It is an adaptable plant, accepting a wide range of altitude, and it blooms through many months of the year. Because of its qualities it might be too attractive to visitors, but it has an effective defense. Its stem and its leaves are thickly armed with small and sharp spines. In addition, the orange-colored juice is deterrent. It is called the prickly poppy.

Massive formations of various shapes rest on an extensive terrace in the desert. Some of them are as high as a three-story building, some only half or a quarter that height. All are alike in their dull-brown color and their rough, flaky surface. The formations are a type of granite, which is weathering away. They are evidence of the fact that an arm of a great ocean once covered the region where they stand.

At the foot of many of the formations a shrub grows, named the southwestern coral bean. From a cluster of strong roots, which penetrate deeply into the ground, canes rise to a height of three or four feet. Some of the group of canes die at the end of a year or two but still remain standing. Others bear striking flowers. When the flowers have completed their part of the cycle, they are succeeded by long pods. Each pod, as it matures, splits open in two long halves, and each half carries a series of beans, which are bright coral red. The beans are separated, one from another, by a tough partition. As the pod opens, the beans are retained in alternate cavities, one on one side, the next on the other. Their display continues through the fall of the year, and is no less striking than that of the flowers.

The southwestern coral bean is not distributed widely, but seems to prefer a location close to the base of one or another of the formations with the rough, scaly surface. Other formations of a different nature seem not to offer the right environment. The conjecture arises that perhaps the disintegrating granite carries mineral elements that the plant needs.

The story goes on. Thirty miles away the same granite occurs, this time in ledges in the side of a canyon. Forty miles farther the same granite again appears. Another fifty miles, and once more a group of precipitous mountains discloses outcrops of the brown disintegrating granite, with deposits of the crumbly rock at their feet. Whatever the reason may be, how it all came about, the southwestern coral bean grows in each of these other places.

It may grow elsewhere. It may grow in places which show no trace of the crumbling brown granite. There may be no connection. The question seems to be unanswered.

Members of the wasp tribe have long since learned how to provide a satisfactory food supply for the start of a new generation. First the wasp constructs a suitable container, making it of mud or other proper material. This is attached to some appropriate object. Then insects are obtained, which are to become food. Each insect is given an injection, which will make it quiet, though still alive. These insects are placed in the container. Finally an egg is added, which will produce a grub of the wasp's own kind. Thereupon the container is sealed. The grub now has an assured food supply, which will remain fresh and will be adequate for its needs. All this is an old and well-established procedure in the wasp world.

In the Southwest you can find an interesting variant of this program. It involves a member of the buckwheat family of plants. All through the Southwest the buckwheat is well represented. Some of its members live in the low-lying desert regions, where they have learned how to survive with little rainfall and to endure heat. Others are at home on the rocky slopes of hills. Throughout this vast region, the family is widely successful.

One of the family's members sometimes participates in an innovation. The main stem of this plant is enlarged in the form of a tall and narrow vase. Not all of the plants in the group do this, but many show the structure.

A small species of wasp has turned this to good account. At the upper end of the vase the wasp makes a hole. Then it collects small bits of stone and drops them into the vase. These serve as a sort of foundation. Next the wasp collects suitable insects, gives them an injection, and packs them into the vase. When enough of them are in place, the wasp deposits an egg. Then it collects more bits of stone and adds a final layer, which apparently protects the food and the egg. The stem of the plant supports the whole arrangement, well up from the ground, out of the range of predators. To the human observer it seems like a good invention.

All through the desert country, as in other regions, the trees and shrubs and lesser plants have developed effective measures for dispersing their seeds. Since they themselves cannot travel to other areas, as can the animals, dispersion must be achieved by other means. The desert is home to one plant that has specialized in an unusual way.

In certain places, where moisture and soil are right, a plant grows which is called alfilaria; in the Southwest it is known as filaree. Its country of origin was Europe. It is an annual, and so dies at the end of the year, but it follows a program that tends to give it the permanence of a perennial. When it blooms it produces long and slender filaments from the base of the blossom. These are attached to the seeds. During the dry period, before the summer showers arrive, the filament is tightly coiled. Then when winter rains come, when the air is full of moisture and the ground is receptive, the filament uncoils. The pointed seed that it carries is pushed into the ground, and in the moist earth it germinates and produces a new plant, in time for a new growing season.

All this works smoothly in the right location. But the soil must be suitable, and the moisture brought by rain must be timely. Like many another device that is accurately adjusted, the filaree's program of preparedness depends on specific conditions. So it comes about that you will find the plant growing well in certain areas, but not in others near by.

Wherever it is present through the successful functioning of its own device, and equally where it has been planted by stockmen, it is credited with being superior food for cattle.

In certain regions of the Southwest country a plant grows that is entitled to a special visit. A National Monument has been set up for its preservation. Although it is a member of the lily family, and is related to the yuccas, it seems to be more like a tree, a strange and almost grotesque tree. Its name, in fact, is the Joshua tree.

It is like an adventurous yucca that has embarked on an endeavor to find out in how many directions it can grow, and to see what it can do in the way of forming branches. As you look at a wide expanse in which there are many yuccas, you can see how the notion might have originated.

The result of the adventure is interesting. As to beauty of form, the Joshua tree cannot make serious claims. It has none of the graceful, curving aspects that we associate with familiar trees such as the elms or maples, nor the sweeping plumes of a pine. Its branches are short and heavy, and look as if they might once have been longer, but had been trimmed off to stubs. A forest of Joshua trees, which may extend for miles, is a collection of curious forms which cannot be graceful. Nevertheless a Joshua has its own claims on interest, no less than a forest of pines.

To begin with, it can do what no pine can do. When temperature and rain are favorable it can produce a large cluster of blossoms at the end of a branch, in the midst of the narrow, pointed leaves. Each blossom of the cluster is white, or greenish white. Each opens only part way, but enough to make a display that is striking.

In the thick array of narrow leaves, many birds like to have their nests. Surprisingly, one of the orioles suspends its woven cradle in the midst of the pointed leaves. The number of kinds of birds in the Joshua tree forest is large, a larger number probably than would be found in the pines or other evergreens of an Eastern forest. Perhaps this may come about because, in a Joshua-tree forest, other trees of inviting size may be scarce or absent.

The trunk of a Joshua is sturdy, and although it is fibrous, it looks like a tree trunk. The branches also are heavy. Both serve as suitable places for flickers and woodpeckers to excavate nesting cavities. After the excavators have used the cavities and moved on, various other birds take over, and so the tree becomes host to bluebirds and wrens, and to small owls. The Joshua-tree forest has its plentiful bird life.

At its foot a Joshua tree fosters other kinds of life. The pack rat secures from the Joshua useful material for its nest. Lizards seek the shelter of the clustered, narrow leaves that adhere to limbs and trunk. On occasion the tree serves the needs of visiting Indians, who secure from it a supply of its slender red roots to use in their basketry.

Making no display at all, in form or in color, the thread plant adds its quiet touch. The plant describes itself with its name. Its stem branches and rebranches, and from the beginning is like a thread, like a strand that was spun by a machine. Next to the ground the plant has a few leaves, but beyond that point the threads take over in an intricate pattern. The tips of the threads bear tiny blossoms no larger than a grain of rice. The whole plant is only a few inches tall.

In contrast to the Joshua tree and the yuccas, the plants known as the gilias, which have many representatives, provide memorable displays in the low deserts and on mountain slopes. One of the gilias adds a dramatic touch. Its blossoms are borne on short stems near the ground. When they are closed they are invisible, because the margin of the closed blossom has the same color as the ground. With the coming of evening the blossoms suddenly open, displaying their broad white petals. Thus, all at once, a snowstorm descends upon the desert, transforming its dull expanse and setting alight the close of the day.

The name of the plant is evening snow.

The Ridge

Many times, on starting out for the day, we have
chosen to follow a desert road that skirts a shoulder of
a mountain and leads to a long, rocky ridge. Invariably,
interesting events would take place along the road, a coyote
flashing across, a band of quail pausing to inspect us and
discover our intentions. Farther along, the ridge offered
its own rewards.

Half a dozen large stalks, light-colored and rigid, stand
up on the skyline as you approach the ridge. Each is seven
or eight feet tall, and its upper third is thicker than the
rest of it, as if it had been wrapped in some sort of bulky
substance. Even at a distance the stalks are unmistakable.
They are the flower-bearing structures of the plant called
sotol, another member of the lily family that gave to the
desert the yuccas and the Joshua tree. The thicker part
of the stalk is the region where countless short blossom-
stems are carried by it, each one of these with its burden
of flowers in summer, later replaced by myriads of seed
structures.

The base of the plant is a great array of long and narrow leaves attached to a thick head. This is the factory that produces the tall flower-stalk and its blossoms, after a long period of preparation for that event. The head does not rise high above the ground as it does with some of the yuccas. The narrow leaf is enlarged where it is attached to the head. The terminal outer inch of the leaf is not a sharp spine but is likely to be split into two soft ends, which look as if they were faded and worn out. Although the leaf is not prepared to repel a browsing animal by means of a dagger point, it meets that situation in a different and effective way. Its margin, all the way along, is beset with sharp and rigid spines.

The broad ridge where the sotols are growing is in itself a striking desert display. Its surface is covered with a rock layer as continuous as if the ridge were plated. Here and there the plating is cracked, exposing another layer underneath, or a seam in the rock surface is not well joined. At these imperfect places the sotols are established. Their roots find a way under the surface layer, and no doubt discover further opportunities as they proceed. Down there desirable moisture must exist, along with pockets of soil.

On the surface of the ridge the clusters of ribbon-like leaves supporting a flower-stalk are far outnumbered, perhaps ten to one, by other clusters slowly preparing for their ultimate fulfillment. In their strength and vigor they are outstanding. The whole ridge is like a sotol preparatory school. In the midst of all this lie the stalks of past years, slowly disintegrating. In their company lie ancient heads that once carried clusters of leaves, but now are only reminders of former activity.

As if the ridge, with its plating of rock layers, represents a special site for desert plant life, the available space is shared with scores of ocotillo plants. Their roots have preempted fissures in the plating, and their wands rise high, some of them higher than the neighboring sotol stalks, some in fact exceptionally high for members of the ocotillo clan.

In the world of the ocotillo, to be out of the ordinary is nothing new. Its very name sets it apart. The name traces back to an Aztec word *octle* and a Spanish ending meaning *little*. The plant requires a whole botanical family for its own use. It has thorns, which are long, curved, and very sharp, but it is in no way related to the cactus tribe. Its long canes, which often reach a height of eight or ten feet, are likely to be unbranched. Several rise from a single base, but they spread out as they go up, and they offer no structure attractive to a bird seeking a place for a nest.

In its own way the ocotillo deserves admiration and respect. Its small and bright green leaves are borne in little clusters just above each thorn. They appear when the plant has had sufficient moisture, and they turn brown and drop off as soon as moisture reserves are exhausted. But the story does not end there. If rain unexpectedly visits the desert and the moisture supply is renewed, a new lot of leaves appear. Presently these follow the first lot. In some seasons this performance may be repeated three or four times.

But again the whole story is not yet told. In times of extreme and prolonged desert dryness, the ocotillo has a way to meet the situation and continue life and growth. Along the length of its canes the outer bark is thin. Beneath it an inner bark is as green as a leaf and is able to continue the functions of the leaves. The whole plant does not turn brown and die. In fact, dead canes are not often found on ocotillos.

In due time, when the season is suitable, the ocotillo has its blossoming period. At the tip of each cane a small and slender spike of bright red blossoms appears, like a flame. During that period, the plant, with its long wands clad in bright green and its vivid spurt of fire at the tip of each cane, is an arresting display.

The almost unending life of the long canes has led to their use in ways that sometimes have striking results. If canes are cut off near their base and are thrust into ground that is moist, they are likely to take root. If they are placed close together and are supported with wire, the result is a living fence. If detached canes are used as an overhead lattice, as a shelter from the hot sun of summer, and if rain comes to refresh them, the canes may come out in leaf and may even produce blossoms.

As if to continue a story of unusual attainments, the ocotillo has played a part in desert rituals. Short lengths of the wands have served as the basis for prayer sticks in the religious customs of some desert Indians. The ocotillo wand is in fact strong and hard. The bark, with its array of sharp and curved thorns, may be removed or may remain. A section eight or ten inches long will be almost straight and will be durable. In accordance with custom, it may be given appropriate decorations and may be placed in some significant and hidden location. Perhaps the singular nature of the ocotillo gives special meaning to its use in a prayer ritual. With its unquenchable life it may well be a symbol of immortality.

Again the story continues, as if the ocotillo had not completed the record of its attainments. In many miles of exploring, here and there in the desert country, we noticed that ocotillos seemed to have a firm preference as to a suitable site. They would be plentiful throughout a certain area, perhaps in a restricted space, but would not be present beyond a definite line.

At this point a friend who owns a currently inactive gold mine agreed to guide us to the mine in order that we might see what it is like. The way led over a rocky desert road, around a spur of a mountain and into a valley. At the road's end stood a rough building, housing hoisting machinery, now idle. Next to the building a deep and narrow cleft in the slope was bordered on one side by gold-bearing rock, while the other side was a different formation which carried no gold.

The bottom of the valley, the slope on the farther side, and the nearer slope up to the cleft, bore familiar desert shrubs, mesquite, creosote bush, and others. The slope adjoining the cleft on the upper side bore scattered specimens of the same familiar shrubs but in addition liberal numbers of ocotillo, growing as thickets in some places. Nowhere below the cleft or on the farther slope was there even a single specimen of ocotillo.

Of course the far-ranging prospectors of past years could not base their search on the presence or absence of ocotillos. Other and more important considerations were the clues. In this case it happened that the presence of the shrub and the existence of promising rock coincided.

The mountain spur that is skirted by the desert road has its own claim on interest. Scattered century plants grow there. They occupy a stony area where the clan must have been on hand for countless years. The patriarchs are there, plants with a central stalk fifteen feet high or more. Some of them must have bloomed only last season, for their stalk still carries the powdery coating of recent life, and their giant seedpods are no more than half empty. Some have fallen and lie across the stony ground like long and tapering wooden pipes. With others, the great clump of thick leaves, dagger-pointed and green, awaits the moment for sending up a flower stalk.

In the midst of all these are the youngsters. Dozens of them, no larger than a pigeon's egg, would seem to be of pre-kindergarten age and not yet started on their active life; nevertheless they display their very small but faithfully pointed leaves. Others, as large as a closed fist, look as if at the right age for grade school; and still others for high school. But all are the picture of a well-ordered century plant.

You wonder how many years must elapse before the very small plants will grow up, and then how many more before a tall flower stalk can come into being. Plants that seem to be full grown occupy places on the rocky knoll. Some one of these may be ready this year to complete its mission, raise aloft its giant stalk, and then wither and die. A nearby plant that seems equally mature may wait for another five years. In its youth and in its maturity a century plant follows its own way. It is the number one conservative of the desert.

In some areas adjoining the desert road the earth is covered with a dark green garment. Over ridges and slopes and across level reaches, the green robe follows every detail, without a break. From a distance, as from a plane or a hilltop, it looks like thick green turf. Nearer, it proves to be bushes, evenly spaced and of uniform height. If the region were in one of the states that is farther north, the bushes would be sage. In the Southwest, the garment is made up of creosote bushes, together with their occasional companion, the burro bush.

The creosote bush tells a little of its story in its name, but only a small part. On a hot day, especially after rain, its leaves give off a resinous, chemical odor. But the plant has much else to offer. It grows well at various altitudes, from regions almost at sea level up to others that climb to several thousand feet. It is not harmed by low temperatures, and it survives heat that many others could not endure. It is able to resist prolonged drouth.

In its manner of growth it is likely to follow an even spacing, which incidentally permits desert animals to travel in its midst. Its visitors can browse on its leaves, if they so desire, although many do not choose to do so. They can seek the protection and shade of its foliage. It does not form an impenetrable, thorny tangle, as do some other shrubs of the desert. Its roots, interlaced in the soil, protect the ground from erosion in times of summer downpours, and at the same time conserve some of the moisture. Individual plants have a by-product to offer. Insects on the stems produce a lac which has served many an Indian family for mending broken pottery and as waterproofing material. Vast areas of the plants offer a striking display when winter rains have been favorable. All come into bloom at the end of spring. A few days later they produce white seed-balls.

The spacing of the creosote bushes allows suitable opportunity for burro bushes in their midst. The burro is a smaller bush, rounded and grayish, in contrast to the dark stems and dark green foliage of the creosote bush. It is a welcome member of the desert cover, for its leaves find special favor among various animals. If the creosote bush might be said to foster the burro bush, the fact could well be entered to the credit of the larger shrub.

Every time that we have followed the road to the ridge, or any other road that makes its way in the midst of untouched desert, we have been impressed by the self-reliance of the desert plants. The shrubs and the smaller plants have an appearance of determination about them. They are like a man who has faced a great emergency, has found a solution, and now rests secure in his accomplishment.

In the desert the individual is likely to be on his own. He must have space around him because his roots must range far and wide. He cannot touch elbows with nearby neighbors. Give him plenty of room and he will find food. He will secure the last trace of moisture from the dry and gritty ground. Let him chance to be in a spot which is especially favorable and he will take full advantage, will grow mightily, and will become an outstanding example of his kind, all because he possesses high powers. A mesquite tree, equipped for finding moisture in ground that seems bone dry, can send its roots forty or fifty feet into the ground in its search; it becomes an amazingly big tree when it finds unusually large supplies. A prickly pear with roots in moist ground will grow shoulder high. All this represents the inherent strength of an individual who is equipped to make full use of whatever resources are available.

In softer and more indulgent regions, where adequate moisture is available and the sun is tempered with clouds, life is relatively easy. In those regions the plants betray this fact in their manner and attitude. They can grow lushly, they can rest upon one another, they ask no isolation, they can be prodigal of numbers, they need no protective armament. The plants of the desert also have an air about them, but that air is not one of ease.

The Open Book

Again and again, month after month, as we traveled about in the desert country, we were continually reminded that in this region the very substance of the earth is revealed. In the canyons and valleys that descend from the mountains, fractured cliffs have fallen away, and the rocks that fell lie beside you, like samples broken off for your inspection. The stream that follows the bottom of the canyon brings specimens from higher regions. If the season is at hand when some of the streams cease to flow while waiting for the melting snows of winter, the rocks and fragments of a preceding torrent are spread out on the valley floor.

Beyond the mouth of the valley, smaller fragments are mixed with water-worn boulders of an earlier flood. Around them and under them lie endless acres of sand, which in itself is a mixed and blended sample of higher regions. In the midst of all this array, known as a desert wash, lie exotic specimens plucked from cliffs. Farther out, beyond the borders of the valley, the deposit continues as desert sand, often with a dry channel running through, as a reminder of floods that cut down through the mixed accumulations of the desert plateau.

In all this lie endless pebbles and larger stones, an invitation to pick up and examine. Although we are not schooled in geology and mineralogy, our quest goes on just the same. If a find looks interesting and promising, if its colors are intriguing, if it has crystals embedded in its substance, it has won its way for its own sake. If in the midst of the sand, small concretions come to light, concealing within their heart unknown formations, a search begins for others, perhaps larger ones. One or more might be cleft with a diamond saw — or perhaps they might be left with their secret, whatever it may be, undisclosed.

In a different region layers of rock tell a story of ancient life. A thin sheet bears the imprint of tiny feet, the record of adventuring by a small lizard a million years ago. Another and heavier layer shows the ripples of an ancient sea, recorded on a long-ago shore and preserved in stone.

If you are schooled in geology and mineralogy, there are no limits to possible exploration and search, other than available time. In a certain canyon, rumor says, there is fire agate to be found. A further rumor declares that geodes, with beautiful centers, can be found in a different direction.

In any case, this is country which is not buried beneath a mantle of earth and vegetation. This is country where in countless places the substance of the earth is an open book.

The desert wind, sweeping down from the north and west, from the south and east, is an architect and a sculptor. The sand grains which are its tools are invisible, except as millions of them sometimes gather together and you see them as a gray and brown cloud. Nevertheless, sharp grains of sand, possessing no direction or power of their own, become active agents when the wind takes them in hand. You cannot see the scope of their work in the course of a single lifetime. Only if your observations could span a century or more could you appreciate their continuous accomplishment.

In the mountains the wind discovers rock strata that have been laid bare, and out of this rock it carves pinnacles and temples. Finding a place where it can do whatever it may choose, the wind removes part of the foundation from beneath a great boulder and leaves it poised as if ready to tip over. In a canyon it discovers a rock wall with layers rising in a sweeping arch. Setting its sand grains to work it removes the softer parts of the rock, leaving in the wall a great sheltered space with arching roof as high as a ten-story building. Countless centuries later prehistoric man used the shelter as a place in which to build his small dwellings.

In the low-lying plains the wind becomes architect instead of sculptor. Finding the sand grains available in countless millions, it pushes them on and on, as if they were waves of the ocean. Encountering a spot where, in an earlier adventure, an obstacle checked its drive, it builds upon the obstruction. Returning again and again, it contrives a sweeping, curving wave that does not subside but remains. Performing this task over a wide expanse, it gives to a broad plain its own architectural design.

In a far-off different region, where the land is clothed in trees and lesser plants, where rainfall maintains the verdure, where soil has accumulated, the wind cannot be an untrammeled sculptor and architect. Only in the desert can you fully see its accomplishments.

In various places of this country, prehistoric man devised his small habitations and lived his life. Here and there he left behind him evidence of his long-ago occupancy. Some day, when you walk across a level bench near the foot of a mountain, or cross a plateau where mesquite trees and creosote bushes seem to have the stage to themselves, you may see at your feet a small flat object, smaller than the palm of your hand. It has irregular margins and appears to be slightly curved. When you pick it up you find that it has an under surface which matches the upper. Its thickness is less than a quarter of an inch. What you have found is a fragment of pottery, a piece of an ancient bowl, long since broken and the pieces scattered.

It is a crude specimen. The bowl never had been smoothed and decorated, but was simply a utility vessel. If you search long and hard, you may find a different fragment, thinner and with a trace of a black design on a dull white background. Somewhere you may discover a fragment that has had a small hole drilled through it near one edge.

Only a student of prehistoric cultures and the civilizations that followed could surmise with reasonable certainty the story of the three fragments that you have found. You can guess that the first one dates back to people, perhaps a family, who had a small habitation not far away, or who made a journey to hunt or secure food. The second fragment with its trace of decorations on a white background, may have come from some distance, having been acquired in trade. The piece with a hole near the margin represents perhaps a bowl that was broken into two or three pieces and then repaired by drilling holes and fastening the pieces together with thongs. The repaired bowl would not hold liquids but would serve for grain or other dry substances.

In any case, the desert has disclosed possessions that awaited discovery. It can do this because of the very fact that it is a desert country. Rich soil and abundant vegetation would not so readily reveal long-ago life. Like the hills and mountains, the ancient dwelling-places in the desert are likely to remain unencumbered by accumulated soil and trees. There were human dwellings and groups of dwellings here and there in many places of the Southwest, especially in the region that includes the deserts and the mountains. For one reason or another, men came there to live, and remained to leave behind them the evidence of their activities.

The mountain that we can see from our window made no promises. It never had made any. From crown to base its surface is gray, as uniform as if all of it had come from the same melting pot, filled with the same ingredients. There is no band of different color, no knob or ridge of different texture.

Part of the surface is made up of fractured rocks that look as if they had come from a giant mill, into which the mountain's substance had been poured. Other parts of the surface, which had escaped the mill, now lie in low elevations, a foot or two high, like giant ribs. In the midst of the rock surface small hollows have given foothold to twisted shrubs, each one a duplicate of its fellows, each proclaiming the fact that searching roots, which had made their way into hidden crevices, had found nothing new or different.

On one of the mountain's flanks, a gully, not deep enough to be called a canyon, descends to the plain below. A little more soil and a little more moisture occupy the bottom of the gully. In this grow larger shrubs and a few stunted trees. Their roots, with more energy at their command, searched more deeply into cracks in the mountain's substance, but found nothing more than the small shrubs had found. The mountain disclosed no secrets.

Then one day came a man who slowly explored the mountain's surface, step by step. He was in no hurry. The results each day were the same as those that preceded. The fractured rocks yielded no clue or suggestion, and the gully was equally unresponsive. One by one the man examined the low elevations that looked like giant ribs. On one of these he lingered, and with the geologist's hammer that he carried he broke off fragments. Then he descended to the plain below and walked to a nearby village.

The next day he returned and brought with him two men and heavy tools. Together they set to work on the giant rib, removing the surface bit by bit, as a surgeon might operate on a patient. Days passed, as a little of the substance within the rib was exposed. More workmen came, and more of the gray rock was removed. Finally the secret was revealed, a deposit of marble, extending to unknown depths, waiting to be excavated.

The mountain had made no promises. It never had

made any. But it was ready to reward the explorer who asked only for opportunity.

At an unmarked point on the highway, an obscure trail leads across a rough and treeless desert bench. No one seems to use the trail. It shows no footprints. Passing over a low ridge, it crosses a small flat and again surmounts an inconspicuous ridge, growing more obscure as it proceeds. Beyond the second ridge it merges on a broader flat valley, in the middle of which a deep and wide gully leads down from a high tableland. A few yards from the gully lies the objective of the trip.

It is the buried trunk of a big tree, lying prone and almost covered by desert sand. Its bark is rough and marked with deep fissures. The gradual curvature is such that the buried trunk must have had a diameter of five feet or more. The length can only be guessed, since it is covered and invisible, but a low protruberance, forty or fifty feet away, can be uncovered enough to indicate that it is a part of the same trunk, seemingly the place where a limb, now gone, once grew.

Probably the higher ground, where the gully has its beginning, was once the site of a great flood plain, now vanished. Somewhere on the higher part of the plain stood a forest of evergreens. At some time one or another of the big trees toppled into a river that crossed the plain. Borne down stream by the current, the tree lodged on some obstruction. Slowly, decade by decade, the silt carried by the river buried the massive trunk.

Then began a transformation. Little by little, cell by cell, the wood of the trunk and its bark became mineralized. The living substance retained its pattern. All of the growth rings remained unchanged in form, all the cell structure was unaltered. But the trunk had become what we speak of as petrified wood, very much harder and heavier than the trunk that was carried along by the primeval stream. If the minerals that displaced the original contents of the cells chanced to be favorable, sections of the petrified trunk might be highly colored. If in addition, the structure was such as to lend itself to the sawing and polishing of sections as thin as cardboard, the trunk might yield the product known as landscape wood, translucent and beautiful.

A plant with a built-in time-scale of its own lives in an open space which we can see from our windows. It is called a joint fir, a name given to it because it is constructed with long joints and because, although a perennial plant, it bears cones, as if it were a member of the family of pines. Living in the present, it harks back to the ages when tree ferns covered the landscape. It has its own calendar, combining ancient times with current years. As if to be consistent, it lives in places where warmth prevails, where perhaps tree ferns might grow today if there were greater moisture.

There are several versions of the plant, occupying various regions, but all have similar aspects. Straight stems, like reeds, rise from a common base. With one version, the stems branch and spread out, producing a plant that may be two feet high and as broad as it is tall. With another version, the stems, although they branch, tend to be parallel and upright, resulting in a plant that may be four or five feet high. In either case a stem is made up of long joints, connected end to end by short, enlarged nodes.

At each node the plant bears two or three very small leaves, which are like green scales. These appear at the traditional time in the spring, when other plants are assuming their foliage. But with the joint fir, the leaves remain for only three or four days. By that time their temporary career seems to have been concluded, and they dry up and fall off. The plant can manage without them, for the long stems are green or gray-green, and presumably serve the plant's needs.

Each node bears also the plant's blossoms, which are as odd as the rest of the plant. Male and female are separate, a plant carrying either one or the other. Each has the form of a small cone, with overlapping scales. In the case of the male cone, small structures in the form of blossoms are borne, with a small scale to guard them. They have yellow stamens, small but prominent. In the case of the female cones, some of the scales serve as the blossom structure. After the female has been fertilized, the scales become the receptacles for the plant's large seeds. These are edible, and when roasted are palatable. They have long been gathered and used by Indians. Also, they are much sought after and gathered by some of the ground squirrels.

In early days the long stems themselves served human desires. Dried, they were used in brewing tea, which pioneer settlers found a pleasant flavor. In early years, also, Indians of the Southwest used the tea as medicine, desirable because of its tannin content.

So it comes about that the time-scale of the joint fir relates to present-day needs and desires, and at the same time to periods in ancient history.

Earth and Sky

A craggy mountain rises from the desert plateau near the house which we occupy. Up there the drama of the desert dawn begins, and the pageant of the sun's entry into the blue vault of the sky is enacted. From our windows, and from the open space beyond our door we have watched that pageant morning after morning, week after week. It is never the same, yet never changed.

Before the approaching sun has risen to the rim of the world, the plateau and the mountain rest under the arch of a blue-black night sky, where only stars give light. The stage is prepared and ready. Slowly, imperceptibly, the hidden sun, poised in the depths of cosmic darkness, touches with its fires the limitless space above it. Slowly, imperceptibly, the mountain peak feels the distant rays quicken its crags. Slowly, imperceptibly, a rose glow begins to envelop the peak's lofty form, faintly at first, then with deeper and deeper strength, until presently the summit is a towering, glowing structure rising above the darkness of the world beneath.

131

Steadily, unalterably, the sun continues its hidden advance. In a few moments its intense fires touch the distant rim of the world. Its unquenchable rays seek and find the mountain peak. The soft rose is overwhelmed by the light of day, and the peak with its crags and pinnacles becomes the rock of its everyday life. The dawn miracle is complete. The drama has come to an end. The lights are turned up on the stage of the world.

When dawn comes to the great level leagues of the desert, the sun sends its rays over the vast space of an unimpeded world. It is the torch-bearer to a hemisphere. The cool, white glow that came from the horizon is now a part of both earth and sky, illuminating the realm of the stars even while it reaches out for mountain and plains. The light that touches the place where we stand, transforming to silvery lacework the nearby cholla cactus, envelops also the candelabrum of a yucca ten miles away. This is a cosmic dawn, but nonetheless personal, a dawn that binds you to the great universe of which you are a part.

In the desert the dawn seems devoid of warmth, and yet is imbued with a hidden celestial fire. It is at the same time both cold and warm. It is silent, and yet it rustles with the crackling of the stars that it has just extinguished. It envelops the world in a garment that you cannot touch, and yet the world is everywhere newly clothed. It possesses no faintest perfumes, and yet in its presence the very light itself becomes the bearer of creosote bush and the blossoms of mesquite. It is as timeless as the far off stars in space, and yet it marks the passage of time. It is universal and impersonal, and yet to you and to all your fellow creatures it is intimate and personal.

The desert sun is unwinking. Its eye remains wide open from early morning until finally a mountain in the west imposes a barrier that cannot be penetrated or obliterated. At the moment, within a few seconds, the great eye of the sun is closed, and only the reflected light from the sky remains.

Within the fixed limits of its allotted hours the sun is supreme. It does not yield to passing clouds, for much of the time there are none. Nothing can deny the sun's omnipotence or detract from its authority. Step into its presence and you are flooded with its light. All the world around you is immersed in its radiance. The rocks and the mountain slopes are explicitly drawn, as if cast in metal. The pointed leaves on the liveoaks are unalterably delineated. The countless thorns on the cholla cactus are made of inexpressibly rigid glass. The branches of the allthorn, immovably fixed in a tangled maze, are cast in unyielding gray steel. Where the liveoaks and the mesquites draw a shadow on the ground, the pattern is as sharply defined as if made of iron. In bright light and in shade the sun rules the face of the earth and all that live thereon.

Everywhere the beams of sunlight bear on their shafts the shining warmth that engulfs the world. No other heat is like this. It penetrates and saturates. Step out of its beams, and instantly you move into a realm that is different. All of the animals of the desert know this. If the warmth is more than they wish to endure, they seek the shelter of shrub or tree or that of a burrow in the ground itself. All of the plants of the desert know it and protect themselves with leaves turned edgewise or with other devices. For all of them, for all living things, the sun is supreme. You bow to its authority.

Animals of the desert know all about the desert sun, and shape their activities in accordance with their knowledge. Take a walk in daylight hours of the summer season and you will see countless tracks, from the delicate traceries of small animals to the deeper footprints of larger visitors. But you will not see the animals themselves. Partly this will be due to the need for hiding from enemies, but also it represents the desire to avoid the high temperature of the ground surface. Burrows under the surface, especially under bushes, provide a cooler haven, and the smaller desert animals make use of this. Through the hot daylight hours they take a siesta.

Some of them go further. There are ground squirrels in the desert that spend the hottest part of late summer deep in the earth, in a state of suspended animation, which is similar to the winter hibernation of other animals in the North. Through the earlier part of the year they do very well. The winter rains, though they may not be heavy and may not last long, contribute moisture to the ground and set vegetation growing. This gives the ground squirrels their opportunity for feeding and for raising a family. As summer proceeds the moisture diminishes. Temporarily, dryness is relieved by summer showers. Then comes a period of maximum heat and dryness, when for two or three months suitable food for the ground squirrels cannot readily be found.

At this point the resort to suspended animation takes place. The ground squirrel goes deep into the ground, closes the door behind him, curls up in a tight ball, and goes to sleep. His body becomes so inactive that respiration barely continues, his need for oxygen is low, and his loss of moisture is at a minimum. Thus he survives the extreme period and in due time is ready to resume normal existence.

When rain comes to the desert country, the display of elemental forces is different from any that may take place in regions of more frequent storms.

In the desert, whether in the low-lying country of sand or in the foothills of the mountains, the surface of the earth is dry. It is not covered with moist earth, or with the continuous plant growth that conserves moisture. The stage is set for a drama of the earth as well as the sky.

If you are standing on a height, you may see three or four different storms in different directions, all at the same time. Each has its attendant clouds above it, perhaps dark, filled with swirling winds and illuminated with the flash of lightning, perhaps gray as if the storm were temperate in disposition. Each cloud bank has beneath it a curtain that extends from cloud to earth. Each is moving across the face of the land, perhaps in accord with its fellows, perhaps following its own program. One of the group may advance toward your eminence, but then turn and go elsewhere, leaving you dry-clad and dry-shod.

In the canyons, a small rivulet of clear water that has found its way over and under the stones for many months, suddenly acquires new life. The rivulet becomes a creek, which no longer is content to disappear beneath a stony bed but now immerses smaller stones and pours over larger barriers in newly created cascades. Instead of murmuring softly, it becomes vocal. The clear water of its flow changes to a turbid current. If the storm continues for an hour or two, little streamlets are born on the canyon slopes. Flowing through dry, loose earth, they join the creek on the canyon floor and bring to it their yellow and brown burden, while at the same time transforming the flow to a torrent. For a little while, perhaps for an hour or two, perhaps for a day or a night, the flood rolls along boulders a foot or more in diameter.

Below the canyon's outlet, a wide and dry area, where sandy spaces are bordered by a rough bed of stones, hears the distant sound from the mountain's flank. Presently messengers appear, small trickles in the midst of the rocks. Almost within seconds the trickles change to running streams, and then to a rushing flood. If a little-used road crosses the wash, the chance traveler waits. The passage will soon be safe. If the road is a main thoroughfare, where motor cars arrive by the minute, day and night, the wash must be bridged.

Over the desert country, the rain finds other recipients than canyons and washes. Almost overnight the desert grasses, which have been only two or three inches tall, raise their spears to twice that height. The mesquite trees, with roots fifty feet in the ground, call on other roots near the surface and freshen their leaves. The creosote bushes, covering many square miles of terrace and plains, wait a few hours for the return of a warm sun and then spread upon the air their own odor which is like the tang of some chemical. The cactus that has seized upon drops of moisture that moved down to waiting roots, stretches its body and arms like a man awakening from a long sleep.

When rain comes to the desert country, the drama that takes place is many-sided, small and delicate even while it is elemental.

The desert is unequivocal. Either it does or it does not, even though it is unpredictable.

If fair weather is in order, the skies remain clear, day and night. The sun shines upon the land in unimpeded strength, and by midday builds up a glowing warmth that envelops everything, even in winter. When the hours of darkness arrive, the earth shares in the crisp chill of outer space. There is nothing half-way about day or night.

If the rainy season has arrived, the skies fill with clouds which cover all the land, from nearby hills to neighboring mountains. For their allotted time, whatever it may be, the clouds rule the earth. The sun has no place. There is no irresponsible byplay between fair weather and showers, no smiling sunlight resting for a moment on the wet and shining face of tree or shrub.

The wind follows its prescribed course. It may blow half a day from the east, the other half from the west, but it does not continually shift around, here and there, as if the orders were confused. It may blow across a dry and dusty region with determined strength, and when this takes place there is no question about its unequivocal intent. Another day it may not blow at all. But there is no fickle vacillation.

The neighboring mountain that you see from your window is not disguised by a cloak of soil or verdure, but is fully and intimately set forth. Its rock structure is revealed. The canyons that extend from its flank to its base are unmistakable. The ridge that is outlined against the sky is cleancut. A more distant mountain, visible in another direction, permits less detailed examination because of the miles that intervene, but it is nonetheless definite.

Close at hand the mesquite trees, the giant stalks of century plants, the candelabra of the yuccas, the spreading wands of the ocotillos, and the pads of prickly pear, stand forth in revealing clarity. If they possess spines and thorns, these are as positive as the mountains and the sunlight.

The desert is unequivocal even while it is unpredictable.

When winter comes to the desert country, it brings with it some changes in the outdoor world, but much remains unchanged. In regions and states to the north and east, snow, either present or threatened, takes command. In the desert the sun dominates. Its warmth is something palpable which can be sought and felt and which immerses everything out-doors. When the sun retires for the night, the chill of outer space takes over and remains until the return of the sun the next morning.

In the evergreen forests of the high mountain areas, snow comes and remains through midwinter, often accumu-lating to a depth of three or four feet. You can see it from the valley. But it does not extend down the mountainside more than half-way, and it does not dominate the life of the valleys and lower regions. If a midwinter storm spreads a white blanket over lower lands, the cover is likely not to remain more than a day or two, and not to be followed by further visits.

Under the dominance of the sun and its warmth, much of the desert's plant life continues with little slackening. Over many miles of level terrace, creosote bushes are as brassy green as in summer, lacking only the small blossoms that they will wear in a few weeks. In their midst, other plants, which have dropped their leaves, retain their twisted branches and their garment of thorns. The pads of prickly pears are active green, merely reminding you that presently they will assume their decorations of gay flowers. Liveoaks in the neighborhood of washes are an irregular solid of deep and unchangeable green. Cottonwoods in their midst have exchanged the leaves that they dropped a few weeks ago for the gauzy promise of a new dress in the making. Thick clumps of joint fir, scattered over a pasture, are as green as if there were no such time of year as winter.

In the world of animal life a brief rest has come to

some members. Gophers in their underground world have remained hidden, but the bright sun with its increasing warmth finds new mounds of fresh earth pushed up through the surface of level areas where stones are not too large or numerous. Ground squirrels inhabiting a big mound come out to renew their quest for food. In the midst of the mounds, jackrabbits, who have not been asleep at all, streak across a terrace at a speed almost too fast for the eye to follow. A roadrunner, welcoming the warmth, sits on a post with feathers fluffed out, taking a sunbath. Quail, singly and in small groups, cross the road at a fast walk. A woodpecker on a cottonwood tree protests the presence of a stranger by complaining in a whining voice. In the sand of a wash, footprints are the signature of whitetail deer and a javelina, for whom winter has meant little change in daily activities.

As winter fades away and spring begins to take its place, birds that have spent the midwinter in some country far to the south, arrive and remain for a few days before resuming their journey north. A week later another flock, a different one, pauses for a while. Others follow, each at its own time. Even when summer is beginning, a group arrives, waits, and departs.

Winter in the desert, never a time of locked-away life, has merged imperceptibly into the full tide of the year.

One day, so the story goes, the wind and the clouds set out to find a broad and far-reaching stage on which they might enact their pictorial dramas together. They had tried a region of meadows and fields, forests and hills, but always a scene had to come to an end before its completion, because the stage was too small. They had enacted the dramas over the ocean, but the stage was always changing, even from hour to hour. Finally they looked down upon a vast desert country which extended for many miles in every direction, even beyond the horizon.

Although the country seemed to be a desert, it was not barren. Here and there liveoaks occupied sheltered spots. Where there was hidden moisture beneath the surface of the ground, mesquites grew in orderly numbers. Everywhere yuccas held aloft blossom clusters, and in their midst shrubs and cactus plants spaced themselves according to their needs. Beyond all these, to north and south, to east and west, stood mountain ranges, like the frame of a vast picture. Beyond them more distant ranges were visible.

For several days the sky that arched over the vast arena was empty. Then one night the wind summoned the clouds. At dawn the sun illuminated a great pageant of the wind and the clouds.

Hour by hour, all through the morning and all through the afternoon, the drama developed, scene by scene, act by act. There were no limitations of restricted settings, no interruptions in the midst of scenes, no break in the sequence of events. At last the drama was concluded, and with its ending the sun descended behind a mountain in the west and entered the bedroom of night.

So it came about that in the desert, the wind and the clouds found the answer to their search. And so it continues to this day.

Index and Scientific Names

142

143